An Imperfect Purchase
Shop Smarter Look Better Love Your Wardrobe

Linda Wolfe

Contents

PART I:
SHOPPING
SCREWUPS

Chapter 1

Wardrobe Woes

WHAT'S WRONG WITH YOUR CLOTHES

W hy is there so much drama and frustration surrounding our clothes? Statistics say that women spend an average of 17 minutes each day trying to decide what to wear. Struggling over our wardrobes makes us feel out of control causing us to experience wardrobe rage. Wardrobe rage is when we have irrational tantrums directed at our clothes and our closets when trying to get dressed. It's estimated that 62 percent of women suffer from wardrobe rage.

What do we do after a bout of wardrobe rage triggered by a closet full of clothes and nothing to wear? Go shopping!

We head to the mall to start looking for potential purchases. After hours of trial and error we finally find a few pieces we like enough to buy. But then, once we get home and look at our new clothes we inevitably wonder why in the world we bought any of it. What were we thinking? We consider returning everything. In the meantime, we'll just put the clothes in the closet until we have time to go back to the store. Three months later, there they sit, with the tags still attached. By then, it's too late to return them.

Or, we pull out our laptop, visit a bunch of websites, and place a few orders. We are excited about our selections. But, when they arrive and we try them on we're quickly disappointed. The fabric is itchy, the fit is off, and we don't remember the color being so bright in the picture. We suspect we'll never wear them, but returns are such a hassle and often an additional expense. So, we keep the clothes figuring we'll wear them one of these days. But we don't. Instead, we find ourselves faced with the same questions:

Why did I buy this?

What was I thinking?

And, why didn't I just return it?

We can't help but wonder where we went wrong. We think we're buying clothes we like and need but then we never wear them. Instead of solving wardrobe woes, most shopping trips only add to the problem.

But why?

But why is shopping for clothes, shoes, and accessories so hard?

So confusing...

So overwhelming...

Why do we buy so many clothes that we never wear?

What are we doing wrong?

These are the problems plaguing many of us. By the end of this book you will have answers to these questions and solutions for how to make your wardrobe better.

At the most basic level, the purpose of clothes is to protect us from the elements and to adhere to the expectations of society. In other words, you can't run around naked.

But, clothes are more than purely functional. They inform others of your personality. It takes about seven seconds for someone to form a first impression of you based on your appearance. Strangers unconsciously decide in just a few seconds whether or not you are successful, approachable, take pride in your appearance, and are with the times, based solely on what you are wearing.

That's a lot of pressure! No wonder we stress so much about our wardrobes. This pressure inevitably triggers a host of feelings and emotions. We think about our body image and our weight. We wish we were taller and slimmer, or curvier and younger.

We wish we had unlimited funds like our favorite tv characters seem to have to fuel their giant wardrobes. We think that money is the solution to our wardrobe woes. But we forget that these are make believe shows and not an accurate depiction of reality.

These days, we also see so called "influencer's" posting about their fabulous wardrobes and all the finds they picked up on their latest shopping trip. It seems like they shop every day, therefore, so should we. But it is important to remember that they are getting paid to promote the pieces they are wearing. They make money whenever someone buys something through one of their links. Or, they get free clothes in exchange for proclaiming how incredible they are and for convincing us that we need to get them too. But we all have a diverse thought process and a unique way of viewing things. We all have different needs, likes, lifestyles, personal preferences, and different body shapes. How can these wardrobe must haves that they show apply to everyone?

They can't and they don't.

If the blogger is a petite woman with not a lot of curves, and you are 5'10" with an hourglass shape how will what she is telling you to buy going to look on you?

The fashion industry is not on our side either. The clothes featured in splashy photo spreads, whether in print or online, are by the same companies that bought advertising space. Instead of providing realistic advice about how to dress for our daily lives, we are shown glossy pictures of beautiful models in designer gowns and sky high heels.

Retailers are working against you, too. They invest a lot of time and money into getting you to buy their merchandise. Many companies hire consultants and psychologists to study consumer behavior and buying patterns. They use this knowledge for the benefit of their bottom line. It is in their best interests to make you believe that you constantly need new clothes. They could care less if you never wear the clothes, shoes, and accessories once they get their money.

A big part of the problem is that we were never taught how to shop. There were no courses in school on clothes shopping. There were no classes about creating a clothing budget or how to figure out which colors look best on us. So, we turn to the aforementioned fashion magazines, online influencers, and blogs for advice on what to buy. But as I just mentioned, much of that advice is for their benefit not ours. When we buy the clothes they want us to buy they don't work for us. This sets in motion the mental loop of wishing we were thinner, richer, and younger, like the models and influencers we see wearing the clothes.

Another problem with shopping is that there are no "right" answers, no "perfect" answers, and no "standard for everyone" answers. Just like the notion that a one-size-fits-all shirt is ridiculous, so too are one-size-fits-all answers. Since there are no right answers it doesn't make sense to follow the dictates of must-have lists. If you like and need any of the pieces on one of these lists then by all means go for it. But don't feel obligated to stick to someone else's definition of what you must have.

There are many image consultants, stylists, and wardrobe specialist out there with good intentions and valuable advice. But you have to be careful with them too. Some are affiliates for the clothes they show. They make money every time you click on one of their links. And just like the influencers, the advice is not customized for you.

On the other end of the "advice" spectrum we are encouraged to find the best deal and never pay full price. Quality and need go out the window when we see sale signs and markdown stickers. The average consumer is buying more fast-fashion pieces because they are so inexpensive. People brag online about their large hauls, or mounds of clothes, they got for a bargain. But they are overlooking the fact that most of it is trendy, synthetic, poorly made clothing that quickly looks outdated and does not last.

You also have to ask yourself how much is enough? How many clothes do you really need? The answer always seems to be more, more and more. Many people argue that they like having a lot of wardrobe choices. While a little variety is good, too much creates confusion and overwhelm. It is visually chaotic. And variety in the form of cheap, poorly made clothes is not the type of variety you should be striving for.

Whether you are into fashion or not, we all have way too many clothes. It makes no sense. Why are we always chasing the latest trends and the newest styles, filling our wardrobes with fast fashion finds that look dated after one season. When our closets are so packed that we can barely squeeze out our favorite shirt why do we keep buying more? Why do why continue adding more and more garments? Why? What are we trying to achieve? What are we chasing? Why are we spending money on clothes for just in case, someday, what if, and an imaginary fantasy life? Why are our closets filled with so many clothes we never even wear?

Often, we find clothes, shoes, and accessories that we love, but we leave them at the store because they're full price. We hesitate to spend extra on the perfect piece even though it is exactly what we were looking for all day. We decide we are not worth it and we cannot afford it. So we don't buy it. Instead, we settle for a suitable, cheaper substitute.

When you wear the suitable substitute you're not completely confident. You feel self-conscious. And you can't stop thinking about that perfect piece you actually could afford if you stopped buying so many other clothes, shoes, and accessories. Nothing compares to the more expensive piece. You wish you would have just bought it. So, you return to the store, but your perfect piece is gone! Going forward, you continue chasing that perfect piece when it was right in front of you.

Some people get sick of trying to find the perfect piece, or even clothes that they really like, so they just give up. They buy anything that remotely works to get out of the store. This ultimately leads to a closet full of clothes that serve their purpose, but do not make them feel confident and pulled together.

So, what are you supposed to do? How can you be sure you will actually wear your purchases? How can you be sure whether or not you should commit to a purchase or keep looking?

Buying the right clothes is hard, like really hard. So many people struggle with it but don't want to admit it because it's just clothes right? What's going on here?

There are many reasons why shopping for clothes is so hard.

First, there is a lot of pressure associated with shopping. Our emotions and insecurities get in the way thanks to societal expectations about sizes and fit. We let our feelings and thoughts dictate our actions. Plus, we are triggered to shop for reasons other than need including for entertainment, to fill a void, or to keep up with others.

Second, are financial constraints that must be taken into consideration. Unfortunately, we don't have unlimited funds to spend on our wardrobes. We must buy food and pay our bills. We need to furnish our apartments and homes, we need a vehicle, and we have kids who also need clothes. These all divert funds away from our wardrobes. Therefore, we must pick and choose. We have to decide what to buy and what to leave at the store.

Third, are the endless options, most of which are not that great. Too many options leads to analysis paralysis and indecision. Despite the overabundance of merchandise, the selections are subpar and not really what we need. The clothes they are selling do not work for the average person.

Fourth, are the ulterior motives of retailers. They are well aware of our emotional triggers and they use them against us to entice us to spend money. Their main concern is their bottom line not the state of our wardrobe. They could care less if we ever wear anything we buy, as long as we keep buying.

On their own, each of these factors make clothes shopping hard. When you combine them, shopping becomes a nightmare.

No wonder we make some bad choices!

But fear not my friends. We are going to tackle all of these complex issues in this book.

Whether you shop too much, spend too much, always seem to buy the wrong things, or don't even like shopping, this book can help you!

The goal is to curate a closet full of clothes you like and will enjoy wearing. And this means shopping. Once you get the right clothes for you in your closet, you will enjoy getting dressed without the stress, anxiety, and drama. No more wardrobe rage.

That's the key: buying the right clothes for you!

In order to do this you need to engage in smart, thoughtful shopping. Because how you are creating, assembling, and buying that wardrobe is the first part of the puzzle. It's the entry gate. This is how you get all the stuff stuffed into your wardrobe.

By the time you've finished this book, you will be well equipped with the tools to embark on smart shopping trips where you only buy the pieces that work for you. While you cannot control the motives of retailers, you can control your efforts, responses, thoughts, and actions. You need to know how to do this when faced with all the distractions at the mall and all the triggering thoughts in your head.

When you feel the enticing pull of a shopping trigger you can stop yourself and shift your mindset. Just by being aware of your triggers enables you to overcome them, ignore them, or remove yourself from the situation by leaving the store or walking away from your computer.

It's important to keep in mind that curating a wardrobe that works for you is a slow and steady process. It's a marathon, not a sprint. There are no quick fixes, no shortcuts, and no easy answers. You need to think about your long-term needs, not just about immediate gratification. You need to raise your standards and change your mindset regarding which purchases are worth the money. Contrary to popular belief shopping is hard work. It takes time and effort. It takes trial and rejection. It takes planning and intention.

Shopping is similar to getting in shape. To do so you need to change your eating habits and raise your standards regarding what foods you put into your body. You also need to create an exercise regimen and get into the practice of working out. As long as you stick with it and are consistent, you will get in shape. Perseverance is the key. But, if you start relaxing your eating and exercising habits, you will regain the weight.

With shopping, like diet and exercise, you do have to put in some time and effort.

Your wardrobe will not be transformed overnight.

If you start to relax your standards your wardrobe will start to expand and refill with clothes you don't like and never wear.

This is where smart shopping comes in. If you want to love your purchases you need to raise your standards. With so many options there is no reason to settle.

Sometimes you just need to do more searching...

Occasionally, you might need to check out other brands or a different mall...

You may think this is a lot of effort to shop. Maybe so. But wouldn't you rather put your time and effort into figuring out how to ensure you buy clothes you want, need, and will wear, instead of wasting time and money buying clothes you don't love and never wear? Aren't you tired of getting frustrated with your closet stuffed with duds?

Let me tell you a little secret: shopping is more fun when you know what you like, what you need, and where you might find it. Shopping is more fun when you shop with a plan and a budget. And getting dressed each day is stress free when your closet is filled with clothes you need, love, and wear.

Shopping is a miserable experience when everything you try on is too big, too small, the wrong shade, and not your style. Wandering aimlessly, picking up anything that catches your eye, is not productive. Trying on a huge stack of clothes that don't fit right is frustrating. And returning home with a lighter wallet and bags full of clothes that you don't really like and probably won't ever wear is depressing, aggravating, and exasperating.

Shopping is not the problem. But *how* you shop can be. The goal is to guide you toward a healthy relationship with clothes shopping. I want you to retrain your brain about shopping and your wardrobe. How?

- by teaching you to how to notice, identify, and overcome your shopping roadblocks and obstacles

- by being aware of what you are really shopping for because it is often not for clothes

- by learning how the paradox of choice creates confusion and overwhelm when shopping

- by uncovering the real cost of your clothes

- by uncovering your buying triggers that make you overspend

- by being aware of retailer tactics

- by raising your standards

- by creating a shopping budget

- by drafting a shopping plan for success

- by evaluating your purchases after you get home

- and finally, by considering the benefits of a shopping slowdown and a purchasing pause

Why is any of this important?

Knowledge is the key to making smarter purchases, spending wisely, and curating and maintaining a wardrobe that works for you. A recurring theme you will keep hearing throughout this book is, any and all purchases reduce your bank account and increase the number of items in your closet. This prompts guilt over money spent and results in decision fatigue when getting dressed. Plus, the more pieces you add, the less special it all becomes.

Do you really need so many clothes?

Do you really need so many shoes, and belts, and tops?

How much is enough? Why do we always think we need more, something better, or something new even though we already have more than enough clothes in our closets? Why are we so dissatisfied with what we already have?

The goals of this book are to show you how to invest wisely in your wardrobe, how to avoid purchasing to "save" money, and to learn more about yourself. Clothes are expensive, and your time is valuable. I want you to get the most for your money and your time. I want you to stop wasting money. I want you to stop buying clothes you don't wear. I want you to stop settling for just okay or this will do. I want you to stop buying poor quality, ill-fitting garments that do nothing for you.

Instead, I want you to start shopping with purpose. I want you to buy clothes you need for your lifestyle and that suit your personal style. I want you to raise your standards regarding your wardrobe and experience a new approach to shopping. Lastly, I want you to think about a shopping slow down and a purchasing pause. Both can be very beneficial.

Are you ready? Let's get started!

But first, be sure to download your FREE An Imperfect Purchase Workbook here. You can also go to https://closetcures.com/workbook-an-imperfect-pur chase/This is the companion workbook you can download and print.

Chapter 2

Misguided Motivation

WHY ARE YOU SHOPPING

D o you ever think about:

- what is motivating you to shop

- what wardrobe dilemma are you trying to solve

- why you go into certain stores but not others

- what causes you to click on a retailer's website

- what motivates you to choose one shirt, dress, or pair of shoes over another

- what is going on in your head

- what is your thought process behind each decision

- how your emotions influence your decisions

- how your lifestyle, budget, and personal preferences impact your buying choices

There is a lot of emotion and psychology entangled in our shopping habits and the clothes we buy. Both our conscious and unconscious mind plays a role in our emotions. In turn, these emotions impact our choices about which clothes to buy. Why are there so many emotions tied into our clothes? Because we put clothes on our bodies. What we choose to wear impacts how we feel. Clothes can make us feel different ways.

They impact your mood.

They impact how you act.

And they impact how others perceive you.

Clothes can help us to feel authoritative, attractive, or cool. And, we hope, they make others think that about us as well. This is known as enclothed cognition. The technical definition is that clothing impacts human cognition due to both the symbolic meaning and the actual wearing of the attire. In other words, the clothes you choose to wear impact your psychological processes. Clothes affect your thoughts, for better and for worse.

In order to make smart decisions when shopping it is important to identify *why* you are shopping. If you are shopping for a true need then that is the motive. However, we often shop for reasons other than a need. In fact, clothes shopping is often about everything but clothes.

We use shopping to distract us from our problems and our daily life.

We shop because we are bored, upset, or angry.

We use shopping as a method of stress relief.

Or, because we are seeking to fill a void.

But why do we think shopping will make us feel better?

Shopping can provide a sense of control. It is empowering. You choose what to buy and where to go. Problems at work? Buy a new outfit for the weekend. Feeling frumpy? Buy a sexy dress.

Clothes shopping can be an escape from your everyday life. You can try on new personas without commitment. Certain outfits can make you feel more confident, sexy, or cool. When you wear certain types of clothes you embody the meaning society ascribes to, or associates, them with. For instance, a black leather motorcycle jacket makes you feel tough and cool, while a button down blouse and pencil skirt makes you feel smart and chic.

When we shop to make ourselves feel better it is known as retail therapy. The act of shopping releases dopamine in the brain as a response to a perception of a reward. This dopamine creates positive, happy feelings. When we buy a bright, beautiful new handbag we get a rush.

But that rush is only temporary.

Retail therapy that starts out as empowering can quickly transition to stress. This is the shopping and stress paradox. The retail therapy you were seeking to make yourself feel better ends up causing stress over buying things you don't need, sometimes cannot afford, and usually don't even wear because they do not reflect your true style.

We also shop for new clothes because we believe that the new clothes will help us to become the person we want to be. Wearing certain clothes can help us assume the persona we desire. We are buying clothes for the hope of what will happen when we wear them. We aren't just buying a dress. We are hoping that sexy dress will help us find the man of our dreams. We buy a sleek black suit in the hopes it will help us to get a promotion.

While clothes truly can do a lot for us, at the same time, they can only do so much. We have trouble with our wardrobes because we have unrealistic expectations about what exactly these clothes will do for us. And when those expectations don't come to fruition we blame our wardrobe. While that sleek black suit is empowering you have to back it up with actions. You won't get a promotion just because you look smart and pulled together. It might help, but you still have to do the work and prove you are ready to handle the position. You won't land the man of your dreams just because you are wearing a slinky dress. In fact, you might attract men that are all wrong for you.

Clothes can also do the opposite. Rather than empower us, they can make us feel less than, unattractive, or boring. We feel embarrassed if caught in our sweats at the store. If our clothes are ill fitting causing us to fuss the entire day we have trouble focusing on everything else.

While clothes don't have meaning, we as a society, ascribe meaning to them. These meanings impact our purchasing decisions. They impact whether we are making smart choices or misguided ones. This is why the clothes we choose to buy and wear are important because our clothes say all kinds of things about us to others. We judge people instantly, and often without realizing it, because it only takes seven seconds to form an impression. How a person is dressed impacts our view of them because our individual personalities influence all of our clothing choices.

In a flash we decide whether someone is neat or unkempt, whether they care about their appearance or just threw on any old thing. A person's outfit might suggest that they are trying too hard, or not trying hard enough. Some wish to conform and blend in, others want to be unique and stand out.

We gain insight into an individual's outlook thanks to their outfit. If they are wearing a leather jacket, Metallica concert t-shirt and jeans, we will form a different opinion of them than someone dressed in a Garth Brooks t-shirt, cowboy boots and a denim mini skirt. We will associate their outlook with that of those communities.

How we feel about our clothes is also based on whether they function properly. Does your winter coat look fabulous but doesn't keep you warm? Then this will be an issue every time you wear it. Any positive emotions you get from the style will be negatively overshadowed by the fact that you are freezing.

The opposite is clothes that serve a function but are unflattering. If you go to the gym in old baggy sweats and an oversize t-shirt you can still work out. But you'll feel slovenly and uninspired, especially when you see everybody else in their sleek workout clothes.

Why do we stress so much and place so much emphasis on what we wear?

Why do we worry about the opinions of strangers? And of our friends, family, and co-workers?

Who exactly are we trying to impress? Strangers at the grocery store? Friends and family who should love us regardless of our clothes? Co-workers in similar positions making the same amount of money who wonder how we can afford pricey designer clothes and they cannot?

Our shopping habits and purchasing decisions are influenced by the culture in which we live, our social interactions, our personal thoughts and feelings, and our psychological reasoning. We are a materialistic society of consumers who always wants more and better. When we buy things for the purpose of impressing others or making them jealous this is referred to as conspicuous consumption. When we buy the latest and the greatest because a celebrity, magazine, or retailer says they are "must-haves" that is conspicuous consumption.

Media also feeds these expectations. We think everyone else has glamorous lives that require extensive wardrobe thanks to television shows and Instagram. If we see someone in a new outfit or carrying a designer handbag we often feel jealous. Why should they be the only ones to have expensive, trendy pieces? This induces the urge to splurge.

Thanks to makeover shows we believe a new wardrobe will change our lives. All it takes is one marathon shopping session and our life will be perfect. But, one single shopping trip is not going to dramatically change anyone's life. It takes a series of shopping trips for true transformation.

We forget that tv and movies are not reality. We enjoy seeing characters in fabulous outfits despite the fact someone with their job could never afford that wardrobe in real life. If they showed how people really dress it would not be as glamorous. Think of Carrie Bradshaw on Sex and the City. She wrote one newspaper column a week, yet was always wearing Manolo Blahniks and carrying Louis Vuitton bags.

Conspicuous consumption is not a new thing. Thorstein Veblum coined this phrase way back in 1889 in his book *the Theory of the Leisure Class*. At that time, the middle class was developing and more people had disposable income which they spent on unnecessary goods and services. They wanted to show that they could afford it. We still do the same thing today.

We may think that by wearing designer clothes or a monogrammed Louis Vuitton bag that everyone is impressed. We think everyone is thinking how chic we are, and how much money we must have. We can afford it. We must be successful.

I've got news for you. Many people are not impressed. In fact, some may feel you are paying the brand to advertise for them. What a neat trick! They get you to buy something with their logo displayed for all to see.

Old money people appreciate the quality. They may well be wearing designer clothes but they don't need to advertise it because they have plenty of disposable income and can buy whatever they want. And they are not impressed by anyone's blatant display of wealth. But it isn't even wealth. A lot of times people are in debt over their purchases. For all we know, they can't afford the fancy cars, big house, and designer duds that they enjoy flaunting.

Conspicuous consumption can also lead to imposter syndrome. Society praises those who have achieved success, wealth, and power, therefore, we put pressure on ourselves to appear successful, wealthy, and powerful. If we are dressing the part without the success, wealth, and power to back it up we may feel like an imposter. When we buy things in an attempt to impress others, rather than because it is a true want or need, we waste money. This is when we feel like a phony or a fraud. If we charge a designer dress because we didn't have the cash to pay for it we may feel like an imposter.

How you choose to dress conveys your personality and the perception you want to give to others. Brand perception plays a role in purchasing decisions. It impacts how much you are willing to spend, and whether you will be proud to wear something. What attracts you to a brand? Their logo, their image, an ad you saw? Their reputation? Why are you drawn to one brand over another? What makes you shop at L.L. Bean instead of Eddie Bauer or Patagonia? Why do you prefer Macy's over JCPenny? Or J. Crew over Ann Taylor?

A company's marketing, who they select as models, whether or not celebrities wear it, and their reputation all factor into brand perception. Do you buy clothes because you like them or because you like the message they send?

Maybe it's both.

If the commercials and print ads feature a sexy model you believe you will also be sexy if you purchase the clothes.

If the model is cool and in an urban setting, you, too, will be cool and urban if you purchase their clothes, even if you live in the middle of nowhere.

Let's say you are in the market for a new tweed jacket. You can buy one from an expensive high fashion brand like Chanel, or a similar, yet incredibly less expensive, version from J. Crew. Why might you choose to pay more for the Channel jacket? The brand perception. What is the brand perception of a Chanel jacket? French fashion, high price tag, high style, luxury, status, haute couture, an elite club, and something to aspire too. But, J. Crew is also know for high quality. What is going on in your head when you consider purchasing a Chanel jacket? What makes you consider the Chanel jacket when the J. Crew will do? If you want a Chanel jacket because you love the brand, you love their clothes, and know that their craftsmanship is high quality, and you can afford it by all means buy the Chanel jacket. However, the average person will not know whether you are wearing a Chanel jacket or a J. Crew jacket. Buy whichever jacket will make you happy. But don't buy it just to impress others.

When two items are similar yet manufactured by different brands, with different levels of prestige, and come with distinctly different price tags, it makes your purchasing decisions easier. Purchasing decisions become more difficult when the brands are very similar and have a similar price tag. How do you choose then? Why do you choose a Michael Kors handbag over a Dooney & Bourke? Both brands have gorgeous bags.

Both are affordable luxury brands with similar price ranges.

Both are known for being high quality.

And both are very popular.

So why select one instead of the other?

Because of their brand story. Their history. Their advertising. And their reputation. When you buy clothes, shoes, or accessories you are buying into the story the company wants you to believe. If you wear their merchandise, you will also have the same lifestyle as the models in the ads, and the celebrities that wear the clothes.

Companies actively work on their brand and craft their message through the use of color, design, and emotion. They attempt to influence the buying behavior of potential and current customers. Everything from the models they use, to the settings of the photos are intended to convey a message. Consumers buy from brands they feel an emotional connection to, and they buy based on how others will perceive them when they wear their products.

Designer's are well aware that what you choose to wear sends a message to others. When you wear pieces with obvious logos you are trying to tell everyone something. You want to be perceived as whatever that company's image is. If you carry a pricey Louis Vuitton bag you want everyone to think you are wealthy and fashionable. If you carry a Michael Kors bag you are saying that you are into effortless glamour and are chic, whereas, carrying a Dooney & Bourke bag shows that you have timeless style and value exceptional craftsmanship.

With so many brands and stores you need to pick and choose wisely. Retailer's identities can help you choose where to shop. Brands design with a specific client in mind. If you don't match that client then the clothes won't work for you. Why shop at Eddie Bauer if you live in the city and love the latest trends? This store would not be a good fit for you. While you might stumble upon one or two things, chances are you won't. Your time would be better spent at H&M.

If you are familiar with a retail brand you know what to expect when you visit their store or website. It's the same as when you go to McDonald's or Subway. You know exactly what type of food they sell, the atmosphere, the price range, the portion size, and the taste.

What if you are unfamiliar with a brand? How can you learn about a brand's personality? Just go online and type a retailer or designer's name into the search bar. When you click on their website you'll see their tagline. You can also check out the about us section for a description and history of their brand. It provides insight as to whether they sell fast fashion or classics. You see whether they are more concerned with offering a low price or high quality.

Here are a few examples of brand identities:

- Betsy Johnson is feminine, whimsical, and creates over-the-top designs

- Gucci wants to redefine luxury while celebrating creativity, Italian craftsmanship and innovation

- Eddie Bauer makes apparel, footwear, and gear to inspire and enable you to live your adventure

- Old Navy provides the latest fashions at great prices for the whole family

- Land's End is a classic American lifestyle brand with a passion for quality, legendary service, and real value

- Michael Kors brings fashion from the runway to the streets

- Target tells you to expect more and pay less

Being aware of what motivates us to buy certain things and not others can help us make smarter choices. The goal is to buy clothes because we like and need them, not because we are trying to impress others or to fit in.

In the next chapter we will discuss the endless clothing options and how too many choices complicates the shopping process even when you are familiar with a brand.

Chapter 3
Paradox of Choice

A DOUBLE-EDGED SWORD

A t first glance, shopping is easy. You go to a brick-and-mortar store, look at all the merchandise, make a few selections, pay and go home with your new purchases. Or, you click on a website, add items to your cart, checkout, and wait for your packages to arrive on your doorstep.

But the reality is finding clothes you like and will wear is not easy! In fact, it's incredibly hard thanks to the endless stream of decisions that you must make throughout the process. These decisions begin before you even leave the house.

Where will you go?

Should you go to your local mall or are you willing to drive a few hours to a destination shopping location? Do you want to get in and out, or are you prepared to spend the entire day shopping?

After deciding where to go and driving there you have more decisions to make before you even get out of the car. Where should you park? Which entrance should you use? This can be extra stressful if you are visiting a new mall. The larger the mall, the more difficult it is to decide. You have to choose whether you want to park in a central location so you can run purchases out to the car, or, at one of the anchor stores so you remember which entrance you used.

If it is raining outside should you take your umbrella in? If so, you'll be lugging it around all day. If not, you'll get soaked walking in. What if it is snowing or freezing outside? Should you leave your heavy coat in the car so, again, you don't have to lug it around all day, but you'll freeze walking in?

Once inside the next question is which direction to go? Should you go left, right, or straight? Should you go up or down the escalator?

As you are walking around the mall you have to decide which stores to visit and which to not waste your time in.

Once you choose a store and get inside you don't know which way to turn or what to look at first...

There are so many racks and tables to look at...

Should you check out the new arrivals or head straight for the clearance section...

After finding several potential pieces you decide it's time to head for the fitting rooms. You wonder whether or not to take a few different sizes so you don't have to get dressed again to retrieve another size. You doubt any sales associates will actually check on you to see if you need help. They only seem to be around at the entrance, before you need help, and at the check out badgering you to open a store charge card.

After trying everything on you find a few pieces that fit well. Now, you have to decide if you should buy all of them or just one? Should you buy all three shirts even though you only need one? How much can you afford to spend?

Maybe you shouldn't buy anything yet because you just got here. There is an entire mall of stores to visit. Once you do buy a few pieces then you have to lug them around juggling bags as you shop. Should you keep looking? You can always come back later if you can't find anything else. However, this strategy is only good if you are near your car. Once you get to the other end of the mall you probably won't be coming back.

When you do decide to make a purchase you typically have to wait in line. Inevitably, the people in front of you are taking forever. Finally, it is your turn. I bet you can guess the first words out of the cashiers mouth...will this be on you store charge? "No!" And then begins the sales pitch to open a charge card. After declining three times you finally manage to pay and get the heck out of there.

Now that you are out of the first store it is time to repeat this entire process all over again, and again, and again...

After an excruciatingly long day of shopping you return home with your purchases. As you are putting them away doubt starts to creep in. For some reason you are not as excited about your choices as you were at the store. You start to question why you bought them at all. And you spent more than you thought you would. You briefly consider returning one or two pieces but it is such a hassle. Besides, you might just be being silly. You stick them in the closet and decide to keep them.

In an attempt to avoid all of the decisions associated with going to an actual store many people choose to shop online. However, there are quite a few decisions to make with this option too. If you thought there were too many choices at the mall you soon realize that the choices online are infinite!

Plus, there are two big problems with shopping online: you can't try anything on, and if you need to return something you typically get charged for the return shipping, not to mention the hassle of packing it back up and printing a shipping label.

It is in our nature to think more options are always better than fewer options. Seems to make sense, right? With so many options we should have no trouble finding what we want and need.

However, the converse is often the case. When faced with too many options we can experience choice overload or paradox of choice. The phrase "paradox of choice" comes from psychologist Barry Schwartz. It is such an intricate concept that he wrote an entire book on just this topic. Paradox of choice disproves the theory that having more options allows one to achieve better results because more choices leads to more confusion, more second-guessing, and more regret. This leads to *over stimulation, analysis paralysis, decision fatigue, and purchase anxiety.* All of this turmoil ends in dissatisfaction with the ultimate decision.

Of course, we are beyond fortunate to have so many choices. We have an over-abundance of clothes, shoes, and accessories from which to choose. Stores are everywhere and they are packed with merchandise.

But it's a double-edged sword. With the good comes the bad. The more options one is given the more confusing things become, especially if you want to make smart purchases. And who doesn't want to do that?

All of these options are confusing and overwhelming because there are no "right" answers, no "perfect" answers, and no "standard for everyone" answers. Plus, clothing options are only good if they work for you, are well made, are what you need, and are in your price range. And you must look through a lot of options that you won't like and don't need to find something that you do like and need.

If you don't know your style, don't know what you like, and don't know what you need how can you possibly be expected to have a successful shopping trip? You are destined to come home with a bunch of clothes, shoes, and accessories that you never wear. Why? Because they don't go with what you already have, you don't need them, and upon further inspection after the high of shopping has worn off you realize you don't like.

Further, more options not only creates doubt about the choices you do make, but it also creates doubt about the pieces you leave behind. You wonder if you should have bought a blazer in a neutral shade of gray instead of baby blue. You question why you didn't buy the silk blouse in your perfect shade of purple and instead purchased the safe white blouse.

All of these difficult decisions are a result of the paradox of choice.

Let's look a bit closer at the feelings we experience due to the implications of way too many choices. These feelings feed off of one another further enhancing the stress.

Over stimulation occurs as soon as you enter the mall or a store. You experience sensory overload. Everywhere you look there is a sea of colors and prints, tops and bottoms, and sale and clearance signs. Music is playing and people are talking. It is a lot to take in and it can quickly become confusing and overwhelming. You feel like you're entering a different world each time you go into another store. One store may be lively with bright lights and loud music, while another is soothing with softer lighting and mellow music.

Analysis paralysis occurs when you are faced with too many options and forced to make endless decisions. It creates anxiety. We think we want options and like options but then we wish it was easier. More choices are not necessarily better or worse, just more. Too many choices leads to confusion and overwhelm. You don't know where to go or what to look at. You are afraid of making a mistake, therefore, you don't make any decision at all. Or, you buy whatever remotely works just to get out of there.

Sometimes we struggle to commit to a purchase due to difficulty distinguishing between two or more things that seem very similar. We get tense and anxious. We are afraid we will buy the wrong one, or that once we commit to one item we will regret not purchasing the other one.

It's like when you go to a restaurant with a huge menu that could be mistaken for a book. There are so many pages and so many choices you can't decide. It all looks pretty good. But if you want to eat you must make a choice. And buying one thing means rejecting something else, so choose wisely.

Decision fatigue creeps in when you become mentally exhausted with all of the options. Having to decide over and over again about every little thing slowly (sometimes quickly) results in mental exhaustion.

Should I buy the red blouse or the blue blouse? Maybe I should get both? Maybe neither?

Should I get this jacket or keep looking? Is this really my best option? What if something better is out there? What if there isn't and I come back and my size is gone?

I really like this sweater but it's not on sale. Maybe I should come back next week to see if it was reduced? But I really like it and want it...

The longer you shop, and the more stores or websites you visit, the harder and more exhausting it gets. You become overwhelmed with all of the decisions, so you either buy nothing, buy the first thing that kind of works, or buy something, anything to get you out of there.

Purchase Anxiety takes over once you about to commit to a purchase. You experience anxiety about whether or not you really need it, whether or not you can afford it, and whether or not you really like it.

We also have purchase anxiety about the clothes, shoes, and accessories we did not buy. Remember the huge menu with way too many options? Despite loving your new purchases you can't stop fretting about all of the jackets, shirts, and handbags you left at the mall.

The fashion industry does not do us any favors by having seemingly unlimited options. There is constant pressure on designers and retailers to produce and sell, and produce and sell. It's never-ending. On the surface this abundance of options seems great. However, the reality is we are forced to weed through all kinds of merchandise just to find a few pieces that we suspect will work for us. As the saying goes, you have to kiss a lot of frogs to find your prince.

Many of our shopping issues are the result of retail industry methods. While options abound, at the same time we are at the mercy of the selections given to us. If our preferred styles or shades are not currently "in" then we will struggle when shopping. If we need shorts and all they have is pants we will be out of luck.

One of the biggest challenges when shopping is that stores carry the bulk of their merchandise for the upcoming season long before the current season has ended. Fall merchandise starts hitting the stores after July 4th. Meanwhile, most places won't cool down for a few months yet. If your swimsuit gets a snag or you get a hole in your favorite shorts in August you might be out of luck. It's like when they start playing Christmas music in October. How about let's enjoy Halloween and Thanksgiving before we rush to Christmas?

Retailer's are not doing themselves any favors either. In fact, they can be their own worst enemies. Retailer's have trained us to wait for the sale because we know there will be one. Stores receive a constant influx of new merchandise. To make room for the fresh new arrivals they start discounting the existing merchandise. The relentless churning of more clothes is why there are so many sales. There are simply too many clothes. They want to be rid of the outgoing seasons merchandise once the weather shifts. But as I just mentioned, this can create a problem for shoppers who are looking for a swimsuit in August but the stores are filled with jackets. Sometimes you need to get midway through a season to understand what you really need and want. By then, you will be desperately searching the scraps on the clearance racks.

Let's look at a shoe shopping trip to DSW where I experienced all of these paradox of choice problems. The purpose of this expedition was to get a pair of sandals and possibly a pair of sneakers or slip on canvas shoes. Since I had a coupon for $10 off $25, $20 off $99, and $60 off $199, I thought I might get all three.

I revisited my mental list of likes and dislikes, as well as what I was looking for in each pair of shoes. The criteria for the sandals was slip on, no back strap (it always rubs my heel and I prefer to just slip my sandals on and off), no center toe strap, flats, comfortable, cushioned foot bed, and leather. The sneakers could not have laces (I hate messing with them and they always seem to come untied). Other than that one requirement I was open to different sneaker styles and colors. As for the canvas shoes I was also open to seeing the available options.

As I entered the store I saw tables and racks of shoes everywhere. The vast variety of colors and styles instantly created *over stimulation*. I decided to start with the sneakers and canvas shoes as they were mixed together in the aisles. I tried on a few pairs. However, the aisle and section I was in quickly filled with other people, so I took the two pairs of sneakers that I was considering and headed to the sandal aisles.

After a brief search, I found a few pairs of sandals that I liked and that fit. However, they only had my size in black and I already have a black pair. Despite liking them I decided to pass on the sandals. I was being conscious of my existing shoes and trying not to buy the same thing.

I returned to the sneaker and canvas shoe aisles. After more pondering and trying on, I had four pair in contention. One was a pair of Sketchers slip on sneakers in a light blue fabric. These were incredibly comfortable making them a definite purchase. There were two pair of Blowfish deconstructed sneakers with no laces just holes for the laces. These shoes had an unfinished look, but in a good way. One pair was gray. The other a beautiful blue iridescent pair. I couldn't decide whether to get the neutral gray or the flashy blue.

In the meantime, I spotted a pair of canvas slip-ons by a different brand in olive which would work well with the clothes in my wardrobe. But, it had a slim bright orange detail line going along the bottom. I wasn't crazy about the orange stripe but told myself it was not that noticeable, even though that was all I was noticing.

I really struggled with which shoes to get and was experiencing *analysis paralysis*. I was tempted to get them all but knew that was frivolous. Even though I really wanted both pair of Blowfish sneakers I forced myself to choose just one. I could always get the other pair another day *if* I still wanted them, so I chose the more versatile gray.

As for the green pair I debated about whether or not to buy them. I wasn't 100% certain about that pair due to the orange stripe. I was *fatigued* by all of the *decisions* and just decided to get them. I figured I could always return them.

I got in line with the comfortable Sketchers, the neutral gray Blowfish sneakers, and the olive pair of canvas slip ons. After juggling the three shoe boxes for what seemed like an eternity, it was finally my turn at the register. The cashier rung up my shoes and the total came to $179. Under the $199 needed to be eligible for the $60 off. This created *purchase anxiety*. I took this as a sign that I should not get the olive pair as I was on the fence about them anyway. I just got the Sketchers and the gray Blowfish which came in at $94 after the coupon (spend $99 get $20 off) was deducted. While I was happy with my sneaker purchases I still did not get a new pair of sandals or canvas slip ons.

How to overcome the paradox of choice

If you want to make smart purchases that's when it gets hard, but there is hope!

When shopping, the best way to overcome these emotional roadblocks is to decrease the number of decisions. Make your own rules and guidelines about where to go and what to buy. It isn't mandatory to go into every store. Check out the store directory on the mall website before your visit to plot out your route.

Being aware of what you like and need, as well as shopping with a limited, specific list will help, too. Later in this book we will talk about why you should raise your standards when it comes to your wardrobe. This is a way to create a system for analyzing garments to see if they meet your criteria. It's also important to trust your instincts or your first initial reaction to any potential purchase. I knew that orange stripe on the olive shoes would bother me, but I almost bought them anyway. I know I would have regretted that purchase.

Constantly holding out for the absolute best in the world or always thinking something better might be out there is the cause for analysis paralysis. This is different than settling or making due. While raising your standards and being extra cautious is good, being overly cautious is debilitating. Ask yourself why you are so unsure? If you've done your due diligence, it's on your list, the color works, you like the fabric, it fits properly, you like it, and need it, then get it. When it is close to perfect what is left to debate in your head? And guess what? If you do stumble upon something even better than close to perfect get it as well and then you will have two wonderful pieces in your wardrobe!

As I just mentioned, in the second part of this book we'll talk about raising your standards, as well as creating a shopping strategy that works for you and your budget. We will also go over the importance of analyzing your purchases after you get home. But first, you need to learn how to identify your specific buying triggers that cause you to make unplanned purchases and get methods to overcome them.

Chapter 4

Shopping Weaknesses

TRIGGERS THAT CAUSE BAD CHOICES

S tatistics show that 75% of the time we buy more clothes, shoes, and accessories than we set out to purchase. Why? Because we succumb to our shopping weakness and our buying triggers. Anything that prompts us to buy something we otherwise might not is a buying trigger. Everything from sale signs and clearance racks, to advice from a salesperson or a shopping companion, and even hunger and exhaustion can all induce a shopping splurge. What is the result of these unplanned and misguided purchases? A closet full of clothes we never wear and a depleted bank account.

When we shop our thoughts, emotions, and external influences all play a role in our purchasing behavior. As we've been discussing, what we wear can be very personal because clothes impact how we feel and influence how others perceive us. Whether you are aware of it or not, when you shop with misguided motivation you are highly susceptible to buying triggers. Triggers can be subconscious but sometimes you are fully aware of your personal shopping weaknesses.

We are more prone to shopping triggers, like impulse purchases, while in a physical store than online. Indiscriminate shopping or wandering around aimlessly without any purpose or plan makes you more susceptible to buying triggers. You're easily lured by shiny objects and sale signs causing you to make random purchases without thinking them through.

However, even when shopping with intention and a list it is all too easy to fall prey to buying triggers. Many of these triggers work together against you, therefore, you can find yourself under the spell of several triggers at once. No wonder we buy so many clothes that don't work for us!

What might trigger you to buy?

- lure of a low price - spending to save, it was on sale or clearance, or you had a coupon

- impulse purchases - pieces you didn't want until you saw them, or until you saw the low price

- fear of missing out - buy it now or you're out of luck

- wardrobe weaknesses - your love of a certain item, color, or style

- just in case - buying things for events that may happen, or for the fantasy life you wish you had

- emotions - buying to elevate your mood

- entertainment - buying to relieve boredom

- peer pressure - your shopping companions encourage you to buy, misguided or bad advice from salespeople

- it will do - you get sick of shopping so you buy anything that remotely works, you hate shopping, procrastinate and then are forced to buy

- paradox of choice – indecision, pressure, and fear of making a mistake, so you buy too much

- one-hit wonders – only good for one occasion

- avoidance – shopping to avoid doing something, putting off buying something you hate buying like pants and instead buying tops, use shopping as a distraction

- fantasy life – what you want, desire, or aspire to, but doesn't work for your real lifestyle

- shopping as sport – searching, hunting, shopping for fun stuff, ignoring the basics, shopping for bargains

Let's look a little closer at each of these buying triggers. Once you learn to identify them you'll know how to overcome them.

Lure of a low price

I think it's safe to say that we have all fallen under the spell of a low price. When we see a sign for 50% off or a piece on the clearance rack at a ridiculously low price it is hard to resist. However, a bargain is not a bargain if you never wear it. And you have to wonder...

Why are so many clothes always on sale?

Why are the clearance racks always bursting with merchandise?

And why wasn't anyone willing to pay full price for these pieces?

Were they marked up way too high to begin with? Or, is the quality bad and the design fleeting? Is the style one no one wants?

Discount stores like Marshall's and Gabe's are very popular because they are filled with these so-called bargains. It's their store model. But, where are they getting all these clothes? These are the cast-offs from department stores and boutiques. It's the merchandise they were unable to sell, so they unload them on discount stores.

I, too, am susceptible to the lure of the low price, particularly the clearance rack. That's why I have sworn off the clearance rack. I don't even look anymore. Just about every piece I've ever bought from the clearance rack was never worn. While there is a rush in coming home with a giant bag full of clothes, the high is quickly replaced with regret and guilt.

When considering a purchase based on the lure of a low price ask yourself the following questions:

- Do I really love the piece or just the price?

- Do I need it?

- Where will I wear it?

- How will this contribute positively to my wardrobe?

While everyone loves to find a bargain, it does you no good if you don't need it and never wear it. Do not turn your closet into your personal clearance section. The clearance rack and discount stores are filled with last seasons merchandise and the outgoing seasons clothes. Stop buying last seasons leftover junk. One strategy is to only buy clothes for the current season that you plan on wearing immediately.

Impulse purchases

When you buy things you didn't know you wanted until you saw them this is an impulse purchase. Often, it is a result of shiny object syndrome. You get entranced by a pretty color, a fun print, or a low price, and you decide you must have it. Pieces purchased on impulse are usually on sale or clearance. This is a perfect example of a combination of buying triggers: an impulse purchase based on a low price.

When pondering an impulse purchase ask yourself the following questions:

- Is it lust or love? Is it a fling or a commitment? Will you still like it when you get home?

- Does it make sense and contribute positively to your wardrobe? Or, is it a one-off that doesn't go with anything and you'll never wear it?

- Will this piece add to your frustration when getting dressed?

- Will this purchase trigger wardrobe rage?

The best strategy to combat impulse purchases is to just walk away and think about it until you're ready to leave the mall. By then you might forget about it, or decide it is too expensive, too trendy, or simply too far to walk back to the store. Sometimes you go into another store and discover a new piece that you really, really want, and you forget all about the original thing you thought you had to have.

Fear of missing out.

Off-price retailers like TJMaxx, Ross, and Burlington specialize in the treasure hunt model which features an ever-changing, yet limited, assortment of merchandise. You never know what you will find. If you don't get it today it probably won't be here tomorrow. This creates a sense of urgency and the fear of missing out. To keep customers coming back they must have the occasional high demand item or too good to be true deal on a designer piece to provide the necessary reward. Meanwhile, the rest of their offerings are unwanted merchandise from mainstream retailers.

Before hitting the discount stores think about the reason you are going:

- Do you really need something or do you want to make sure you aren't missing out on a treasure?

- Do you actually wear clothes you've bought there in the past or do they collect dust in the back corner of your closet?

- Are you focused on finding a deal rather than on finding something of high quality that you want and need?

- Would it be better for your wardrobe to avoid off-price retailers altogether?

While there is nothing wrong with the occasional clothing expedition to a discount retailer it should not be your main source for clothes. The danger lies in getting caught up in the moment, losing track of what you came for, and buying clothes you'll never wear. If this is one of your buying triggers it might be best to avoid these stores altogether.

Wardrobe weaknesses

When you really love a certain style of clothing and find it almost impossible to pass up that is a wardrobe weakness. For instance, if you fall prey to the lure of animal prints, regardless of the fact the you already have more than enough, that is your wardrobe weakness. Perhaps your wardrobe weakness is an entire category, like shoes. You can never get enough. Or, maybe you can't resist blazers and have them in every style and color imaginable. For example, I am always drawn to stripes and I love the color blue. I think it comes from my love of the water and all things nautical. I also love t-shirts. So, a blue striped t-shirt is almost impossible for me to resist!

Before caving to your wardrobe weakness think about the following:

- How may of this particular item or style do you already have in your packed closet?

- Do you wear all of these similar pieces? Or do you always reach for a few favorites, while the remainder are never worn?

- What, if anything, is so special or different about this piece from the ones you already own? Does it have a different neckline, sleeve length, or some other feature that makes it slightly different?

- Do you really need another one of this item or do you have enough?

Wardrobe weaknesses are not necessarily a bad thing. When you know what you like, they have your best shades, and it is a quality basic that you will wear all the time, such as a perfectly fitting t-shirt, it can be smart to stock up. However, the danger is in spending your entire clothing budget on these pieces at the expense of not buying other clothes you want and need. You also run the risk of buying duplicates or very similar items. For a well-rounded, well-functioning wardrobe it's best to have a little variety in the styles of clothes you wear.

Just in case

While it's good to be prepared, buying and keeping clothes in anticipation of events that may never happen is a recipe for a closet full of clothes you never wear. Having a few basics on hand, like a neutral colored sheath dress, or trousers and a jacket, is smart as they may be worn for many scenarios. But buying a slinky red dress in case you want to go out for a night on the town may not be a wise purchase. Nor is investing in high quality hiking boots when you live in Florida and spend all your time on the beach. The dress and boots are more for your fantasy life than the sheath dress which could be worn for an unexpected event like a funeral.

Before committing to any purchase think about:

- Where you will wear it in the next week or so?

- How often you are likely wear it in the future?

- Do you even have a specific event or place in mind where you will wear it or is this for some event that may never happen?

- Is this the best use of your hard-earned money or are their other clothes, shoes, and accessories that will serve you better?

Buying clothes, shoes, and accessories for situations that may never happen will only clog up your closet and deplete your bank account. Spend your money on pieces you want, need, and will wear immediately. The only "just in case" clothes you might want to have are for situations that might actually happen suddenly like a funeral. For most events, like a wedding or a holiday party, you should receive enough notice to go shopping for an outfit if you don't already have one.

Emotions

Your mood and mindset absolutely impact the quality of your purchases and influence your decision making process. As I mentioned earlier, many people go shopping in an attempt to make themselves feel better. But shopping while depressed or irritated can heighten these negative feelings rather than soothe them. If you're feeling down about your weight or appearance shopping can make it worse because you won't like anything. You will become even more depressed and irritated. Nothing will look good and you won't be drawn to anything. If a pair of pants doesn't fit right you immediately go into self-sabotage mode.

Before making an unplanned purchase when in a foul mood ask yourself:

- Will I still like this tomorrow when my mood shifts?

- Do I want and need this or am I trying to make myself feel better with retail therapy?

- Will I regret this purchase later?

- Does this purchase work with my existing wardrobe?

Making bad purchases will also result in a bad mood later when you see the error of your ways. Avoid shopping when emotional, hungry, tired, stressed, or irritated. If you are in the middle of a shopping trip and you become any of the above, take a break, or simply leave and call it a day.

Entertainment

I'm sure we've all been bored and went shopping for something to do. We tell ourselves we are just looking. This is not necessarily bad if you are capable of just window shopping. However, it is often too tempting to walk away without purchasing anything at all. And as I keep repeating, buying things you don't need and really don't even want leads to a disjointed closet full of unworn clothes.

When shopping for entertainment ask yourself:

- Will this piece still amuse me later?

- Do I have a need for this?

- Do I really want it or is it just a temporary distraction?

- Is my shopping companion pressuring me to buy this?

Instead of heading to the mall or surfing the stores online when bored do something else like go for a walk, read a book, watch a movie, or organize your closet. This buying trigger often works in conjunction with our next trigger: peer pressure.

Peer pressure

Many people enjoy shopping with others. However, you must be careful. While
not intentional, others do not always have
your best interests in mind. They might
be encouraging you to buy more to make
themselves feel better about their excessive
purchases. Sometimes, they inadvertently project their style, their likes, and their
needs into your purchases.

When shopping with others consider the following questions:

- Do you feel less than confident in the piece but others are painting a different picture?

- Can you comfortably afford the piece or will it be a stretch or need to be charged?

- Is it your style or the style of your shopping partner or sales associate?

- Is it your best color or a shade your shopping partner loves?

Being confident in your own likes and personal style will help you fend off peer pressure. Take the advice of others with a grain of salt. Find other activities to do with friends like playing pickle ball, going for a hike, or meeting for lunch. If you do go shopping with others limit your purchases and the amount you spend.

It will do

Sometimes, we get sick of shopping and just want to get out of there. But, we can't leave the mall empty handed because we don't want to come back, so we buy the next thing that remotely works. *It will do* is not a good reason to pull out your wallet. Chances are good that you will never wear it. If you do wear it you probably won't feel your best. Think about how you'll feel wearing a dress that serves the purpose of modesty but that you don't necessarily like. Shopping can be incredibly frustrating. However, that is not a good enough reason to purchase something that you don't love and that doesn't fit quite right.

If you suspect you are settling ask yourself the following:

- Do you feel confident in the piece, or do you feel like an imposter?

- Does it fit well, or are you overlooking something that will bother you when you wear it for more than two minutes?

- Do you really like it, or is it just okay?

- Does it work with your existing wardrobe, or will you need to buy other pieces to make it work?

Later in this book we'll discuss raising your standards when it comes to purchasing decisions. Any shirt, jacket, or pair of shoes that does not meet your high standards should be left at the store. Don't settle just to get out of the mall.

Paradox of choice

In the last chapter we talked about the problems that come with having too many choices. The fear of buying the wrong thing, as well as the fear of missing out, can complicate your shopping trip.

When debating between two or more items think about:

- Which pieces you want and need the most?

- Which shades and colors will work best with your existing wardrobe?

- Whether you really need two or three versions or will one suffice?

- Whether you need any of the pieces at all?

The choices at the mall and online are endless. Therefore, you must shop with focus and a plan to avoid succumbing to the debilitating situation of paradox of choice. If something is not on your list keep moving. Don't be swayed by shiny objects and sale signs.

One-hit wonders

These are clothes, shoes, and accessories that you buy, wear once, and then never wear again. Typical reasons you might purchase a one hit wonder are an upcoming wedding, a vacation, or a date. While you might dazzle everyone at the event, afterwards, the piece gets relegated to the back of your closet.

Before buying an outfit for a specific occasion ask yourself:

- Do I already have something at home that would work?

- How important is this event?

- Am I spending too much on this outfit for this one occasion?

- Do I envision a future scenario where I would actually wear this again?

If you really don't have anything to wear for an upcoming event or you simply feel like treating yourself don't spend too much. Renting an outfit for the occasion or situation could be a good alternative to committing to a new purchase.

Avoidance

When you despise buying certain clothes, like pants or bras, you tend to put it off. Rather than shop for your needs, you allow yourself to get sidetracked by the fun stuff, like handbags and shoes.

As you are walking around the store keep these questions in mind:

- Are you telling yourself prices are too high when you just don't want bothered?

- Are you distracting yourself with your wardrobe weaknesses or shopping for your fantasy life?

- Do you dislike the job or event you need clothes for so you keep putting it off?

- If you don't shop for the items you need today when will you ever buy them?

The reality is the pieces you hate shopping for are the pieces you should focus on the most. They are likely your problem pieces. They represent gaps in your wardrobe that need filled because you avoid shopping for them. Pick a day, suck it up, and just focus on whatever the problem category is. Once you fill in your wardrobe holes you will find it less stressful to get dressed.

Fantasy life

You've likely heard the phrase, "dress for the job the want, not the job you have." This advice is based on the fact that clothes can help you feel more confident. People tend to take on the persona of the type of person who would wear that outfit.

If you find yourself shopping for your fantasy life ask yourself:

- Am I really committed to taking up this new hobby?

- Is this purchase for a situation that will realistically happen?

- Can I wear this purchase for several different scenarios?

- Will this purchase encourage me to make the fantasy situation occur or will it taunt me every time I see it hanging in the closet?

Clothes can give you a confidence boost which can help you get out of your shell or to pursue hobbies or situations you desire. But start with just one or two pieces. If more situations arise that call for more clothes then you can get more. Make sure you actually go dancing once a month or work out several times a week before filling your closet with new clothes. Seeing unworn pieces for an unfulfilled fantasy life can be depressing. You should be shopping for the life you have, not the one you want.

Shopping as sport

Many people view shopping as a competitive activity. Even if they are shopping by themselves. Those who shop for sport love to tell everyone about their incredible finds at incredibly low prices. It is a badge of honor.

If you view shopping as a sport ask yourself:

- Are others really impressed or do they secretly think you are wasting your money on a bunch of junk?

- Do you want and need these pieces or do you just enjoy the shopping rush?

- Do you even like what you are buying or do you just like the low price?

- How many clothes are already hanging in your closet with the tags still attached that were part of a shopping as sport expedition?

Viewing shopping as something to conquer or defeat rather than as a way to fulfill a want or need can result in a closet full of unworn clothes. Setting out to get the biggest haul or the best bargain will result in a mismatched, disjointed wardrobe. Shopping can be fun, but only when you buy clothes you like, need, and can afford.

When faced with buying triggers ask yourself the following questions:

Is your goal to get as big a haul as possible? Or, is your goal to get clothes you like and will actually wear?

Are your wardrobe goals to save money and get a great deal? Or, are your wardrobe goals to look and feel your best?

Is your goal to buy clothes that fit properly and are flattering? Or, is your goal to get the best deal?

Are you trying to impress others with your purchase? Or, do you love the piece?

Do you really want and need the piece? Or, are you trying to elevate your mood?

Do you love the jacket? Or, do you love the low price?

Do you have anywhere to wear the piece? Or, is it for your fantasy life?

Will you wear this for more than one event? Or, will it sit in your closet after the event is over?

Will the piece help to round out your wardrobe? Or, do you already have more than enough versions of the piece?

The best way to overcome your shopping weaknesses is conscious clothes shopping. In other words, being a discriminate shopper. This means being present in the moment, knowing why you are shopping, and what you are looking for. It also means being careful and thoughtful with every purchase, and only buying clothes when you know why you need them and where you will wear them.

Once you learn to recognize the specific triggers that entice you to buy, you will stop and carefully think about any and all potential purchases. Acknowledge what is going on and identify which buying trigger is tempting you. Then, ask the right questions and take the necessary steps to avoid making a bad purchase. Weigh the temporary pleasure of the purchase against the pain of paying for it. There's a reason it is so cheap. If necessary, walk away and don't look back.

Sometimes you do think twice about a potential purchase. But, instead of walking away you rationalize with yourself about why you should go through with the purchase anyway. You tell yourself it is such a bargain that you can't pass it up. Meanwhile, you're overlooking the fact that the fabric is not very soft and the color is much brighter than you typically wear.

What can you do to combat your buying triggers? Own up to your specific shopping weakness, acknowledge them for what they are, and then take steps to overcome them. Resisting temptation is hard. But you need to learn to walk away if you want to stop buying the wrong clothes for you. Keep in mind that shopping weaknesses can change over time, as well as with each shopping trip. They are sneaky like that. Therefore, you need to think very carefully before committing to any purchase.

As you have just learned, many of these shopping weaknesses are similar or work together at the same time. Further complicating the situation are the tactics retailers use to entice you to spend as much as possible. Let's dive into these methods next.

Chapter 5

Buyer Beware

RETAILERS WANT YOUR MONEY

T he goal of retailers is to make money, and they will do whatever it takes to manipulate unsuspecting shoppers to part with their hard-earned money. Companies use strategic tactics to get people to buy clothes, shoes, and accessories that they didn't know they wanted and that they don't need. Retailers are well aware of the consumer buying triggers we talked about in the last chapter and they do their best to use those triggers against us. They spend countless hours and dollars figuring out how to get you to make a purchase. Many even employ people who study consumer culture theory, which is the study of consumption from a social, cultural, economic, and psychological standpoint. They use this knowledge to capitalize on our weaknesses and boost their bottom line.

How are you supposed to go up against this?

- by doing your own research and preparation

- by knowing what you need, what you like, and what works for you

- by being aware of your personal buying triggers

- by being aware of retailer's subtle, and not so subtle, tricks and tactics

Before we dive into specific retailer tactics, let's briefly discuss the history of shopping, the evolution of the mall, and how it is designed to attract us.

Prior to enclosed malls and the Internet, shopping was done downtown. There were huge department stores like Macy's, Marshall Field's, and Hudson's, as well as small mom and pop stores that filled in the busy city blocks. There was usually a shoe store or two, a few small boutiques, a pharmacy, a grocery store, a bakery, and a five and dime. There were fewer stores selling a limited, curated selection of items. In the earliest of days, the merchandise was behind the counter. You could not shop on your own and had to ask the store clerk to get everything for you.

As people moved to the suburbs and the automobile became prevalent strip malls sprouted up, typically with a grocery store anchor and a few smaller specialty stores. While not yet a major threat to the downtown they did have a negative impact and marked a shift in the way people were shopping. These strip malls set the stage for the biggest threat of all, the enclosed shopping mall.

Victor David Gruen is regarded as the inventor of the shopping mall. In 1956 Gruen built the first indoor mall, Southdale Shopping Center, located in Edina, Minnesota. It was like something from another world. He left the outside of the mall intentionally bleak and stoic so visitors became transported and amazed when they walked inside. Once indoors, there were no windows to see day turn to night or weather changes. The climate controlled environment was a refuge in extremely hot and extremely cold weather. Gruen did what he could to entice shoppers to stay longer because the longer they stayed, the more they spent.

Gruen used strategic floor plans, the right lighting, distracting music, bright signs, and intriguing window displays to confuse and disorient shoppers. This is referred to as the Gruen transfer or Gruen effect. Shoppers are entranced by all the sounds, smells, and visual stimuli that are everywhere. This creates sensory overload. The intentionally confusing layout causes one to become disoriented and lose sight of what they came for, thus, making the person more susceptible to retailer's tricks and tactics. All of these ingredients work together to make malls a selling behemoth.

Today, malls continue to have this similar vibe, this familiar hyper-reality. Most malls follow the standard formula of a few huge anchor stores, lots of smaller specialty stores, a food court, kiosks, and sporadic seating areas. In fact, many malls have the same stores all over the country. You'll find a Macy's in Texas and Maine, and you'll see a Spencer's Gifts in almost every mall.

But this cookie-cutter mall model is becoming dated. People are sick of the same old format and the same old stores. These behemoth relics are being torn down and replaced with strip malls, outlet malls, and lifestyle centers. People want to be outside, kind of like the original downtown main street. And they want to do more than look at clothes and shoes. They want immersive experiences like movie theaters, gyms, and even classes they can take.

Of course, the Internet has also contributed greatly to the shakeup of traditional shopping methods. You no longer have to travel to the mall, fight traffic, and find a parking spot, then spend your day trekking through a gigantic mall lugging purchases along the way. Instead, you can shop from your couch in your sweatpants at any time of the day or night.

Before the Internet there were ways to avoid the mall. You would get catalogs and flyers in the mail tempting you with glossy pictures and amazing sales. Online shopping is the modern version of the catalog and retailers have found many ways to tempt you online. Today, your browsing and purchasing is tracked. Ads pop up on your computer screen and phone from companies you've previously looked at. They show you items you are likely to like based on your browsing and purchasing history. And they have popup coupons to entice you to make a purchase. This is known as targeted temptation and it can make it hard to slow down your shopping.

Let's take a closer look at these subtle yet effective methods that make up the Gruen transfer leading you to increase your purchasing.

Layout

First, there is the interior of the mall or the common areas. Here, you will find benches, skylights, and water features. This is also where you see all of the individual storefronts, the store name, and their display windows. Have you ever noticed how the stores are ordered? There is no order. They seem to randomly be placed wherever, with no reasoning. Rather than have all of the shoe stores lumped together, all of the women's clothing stores lumped together, and all of the jewelry stores lumped together, they are a hodgepodge. But why? Wouldn't it make more sense to put all similar stores together for ease of shopping? Of course! But that would not require you to walk past other stores that may tempt you to stop inside. Retailers want you to walk from one end of the mall to the other. They want you to pass Auntie's Anne's pretzel stand in the hopes that you cannot resist. They want you to pass the toy store so your child will beg you to take them inside and buy them something.

As for the interior layout of many stores, it too is intentionally confusing. Kind of like an obstacle course. You see all kinds of merchandise, like brightly colored sweaters, shiny jewelry, and boldly patterned jackets that cause you to experience sensory overload. You quickly forget what you came for and fall under the spell of impulse buys.

Once you think you know the layout they change it! Every retail store I ever worked in was constantly rearranging everything. Racks were moved from the front to the center, clothes were switched from a circular rack to a four-arm waterfall rack, and marked down merchandise was moved from the aisle to the back wall. The reasoning is that these moves make the merchandise look fresh. It keeps you coming back to see what's new and what you might have missed on your last visit. They also want the full price new arrivals front and center. This exposure to different merchandise is designed to increase sales.

Lighting

Lighting has a direct impact on our mood when shopping. It can infuse us with energy or create a calming environment. Lighting can be used to convey a brand's aesthetic. It can denote an upscale store, like Nordstrom's, or a big box discount store, like Walmart. Generally, the more inexpensive the merchandise, the brighter and less elaborate the lighting as this is thought to induce impulse purchasing. The more expensive and upscale the store, the more intricate the lighting. Dimmer, softer light is relaxing and encourages browsing. Jewelry stores use spot lights to make their merchandise sparkle and shine. Designer handbag displays typically feature cubbies with accent lighting to showcase the bags.

Most stores use a combination of lighting to enhance the merchandise which, in turn, aids in increasing sales. Accent, decorative, ambient, and task are four types of lighting that are typically used together. Depending on the type of lights and their placement your attention will be directed toward specific displays, individual products, signs, and architectural features. Lighting can guide you throughout the store, enticing you to explore different sections.

Music

Music stimulates the center of the brain resulting in a psychological, subconscious impact on your mood. Companies use music that aligns with their brand identity and the experience they want the consumer to have while shopping in their store. The ambiance is influenced by the music. It must match the brand. Jazz and classical music is often used in stores with high ticket items like jewelry.

Music is also used to drive sales and can influence how much or how little you spend. Slower music encourages browsing, while faster music gets you in and out. Mild, yet upbeat, music is the most common to inspire purchases. When music is too loud and jarring it can chase people out of a store. However, if it is too slow and depressing it can make people tired and also chase them out of the store.

Displays

Retailers employee merchandisers to come up with floor plans and displays that are consistent in every one of their stores. You can walk into a Dick's Sporting Goods in any city and see a similar, if not identical, layout. However, stores with the treasure hunt model, like Home Goods or Gabe's, have such an unpredictable, random assortment of merchandise, they are unable to have a consistent look and feel.

Window displays convey the brand message and the store atmosphere, attempting to attract their target customer to enter the store. Inside, floor stands, counter stands, end caps, the walls, and even the checkout counter display the merchandise. These areas are often enhanced by different types of lighting as we just discussed. Racks can be arrange by color, category, or entire outfits. Mannequins are used to display complete outfits in combinations the shopper may not think of on their own. They hope the shopper will buy all the pieces. When they see the cool cross body bag with the sweater, jacket, and jeans they want it all.

Store employees

In general, salespeople are not taught anything about how clothes should fit or look. They are just taught how to sell. Sometimes they aren't even taught that. They are just taught to operate the cash register. Since most sales staff are not paid very well there is no real incentive to be helpful, unless they are on commission. Then, they are highly motivated to persuade you that everything looks great and that you need several additional pieces to complete your purchase. Therefore, you should not rely on the advice of a salesperson when contemplating a purchase.

Sales

I've saved sales for last because it is the most triggering of all triggers and retailers know it! When you see those signs promoting new markdowns, clearance, or last chance it sets off alarms in your brain. These signs are meant to create a sense of urgency and fear of missing out because if you don't scoop it up now it probably won't be here later.

Sales serve a few purposes, none of which is designed to benefit the consumer. Despite what retailers would have you believe, sales are designed to aid the retailer. Think about it, they don't need to put the pieces on sale that actually sell.

The reality is stores have sales to:

- inject life into slow moving merchandise

- unload unwanted merchandise

- make room for new arrivals at full price

- lure you in hoping you'll buy some full priced items

- lure you in hoping you'll come in for a "haul"

- encourage you to buy extras in multiple colors

- increase overall sales numbers

Retailers hope to entice you to buy more than you planned on buying, like when t-shirts go on sale. You only need one, but you figure you might as well stock up while they are on sale. Markdowns are different than sales. Once something gets marked down, the price won't go back up. This can spark the fear that if you wait, it will be gone, which is why end of season sales and bursting clearance racks can be very triggering.

But think about it. Why are these items so cheap? This is everything that no one wanted all season because they are usually synthetic fabrics, outlandish patterns, weird colors, and unflattering cuts. Stores need to get rid of them, so they are trying to unload them on shoppers who are triggered by clearance prices. They don't care if they look unflattering on you or if you never wear them. They just want them off of their books. And it gives a slight boost to their store sales at the same time. Win win for them; loose loose for you.

All of these seemingly subtle methods work together to impact your purchasing decisions. If you want to beat the retailers at their own game do not be swayed by their tactics. Being aware of retailer tactics, as well as your own buying triggers, is the key to overcoming them.

I'm sure we've all bought a deeply discounted piece with every intention of wearing it in six months when the weather shifts again. But, guess what? We usually don't wear it. Instead, we want something different, something new, or our likes and needs change. You are better off saving that money until the weather actually changes and purchasing something you are excited to wear immediately.

Cost is important but it cannot be the sole determining factor. Rather, it should be the final consideration. If a garment sits in your closet, unworn, it doesn't matter how great of a deal it was. A bargain is no bargain if you never wear it. Instead, it's just a waste of money and space.

In the next chapter, we're going to see how much you've actually spent on the clothes hanging in your closet. Warning: the results may shock you.

Chapter 6

Down the Drain

MONEY WASTED ON UNWORN CLOTHES

Y our wardrobe is a major investment. Do you view it that way?

Most people don't because we buy a few pieces here and a few pieces there. We tell ourselves that we're not spending that much. When we purchase big ticket items, like furniture or a car, we see the grand total. But when we buy pieces one at time, like we do with clothes, shoes, and accessories, there is no grand total. And when we buy pieces on sale, with a coupon, or on clearance, we justify the purchase by the low price. How can we possibly pass it up? It doesn't cost that much.

But we are spending a lot because it all does add up. Even if the purchase price is low, all those little purchases add up to a big total of hard-earned money spent. And what's more troubling is when we spend our hard-earned money on clothes we never end up wearing! Have you ever thought about how much you've spent on all the clothes, shoes and accessories that are currently in your closet? And not just the clothes you wear, but the ones you never, ever wear? Pieces that you wear are a good use of your cash. However, pieces that you never wear are, quite bluntly, a complete waste of money.

How much have you spent on clothes that never get worn?

Are you afraid to think about it?

While it can be shocking, embarrassing, and downright depressing, being aware of how much money you've spent on your wardrobe can be a real wake-up call. Since you don't want to keep throwing money away this knowledge forces you to raise your standards.

But the real cost of your clothes goes beyond dollar amounts. Beyond the financial implications are the wasted time, anxiety, and added stress that go along with a closet full of more clothes than you could possibly need.

How much time did you spend shopping for all of these clothes?

How much time have you wasted digging through your closet?

How much effort have you put forth and how much energy have you used?

How many bouts of wardrobe rage have you experienced?

What about the mental stress that comes with a closet full of clothes and a depleted bank account? Every time you look at clothes with the tags still attached you feel guilty and depressed.

A rough estimate

If I were to ask you how much money you've spent on clothes this month, this season, or this year would you have any idea? What about the total you've spent on all of the clothes, shoes, and accessories currently in your closet? How about the total spent over your lifetime?

But, you've had most of these clothes for years. How can you possibly remember how much they cost?

While you surely don't remember exact amounts, you should have some idea. You know whether you only buy things on sale, or whether your tastes run toward more expensive, designer brands. At the very minimum, you can assign a *very* conservative dollar amount of ten dollars for every single item in your closet. Multiply that by the number of pieces you currently have, and **you will be in for a shock**.

Let's say you have twenty t-shirts, and let's say you paid $10 per t-shirt. That is $200.

Now, let's say ten of those t-shirts cost $15 dollars.

10 x $10 = $100

10 x $15 = $150

You would have spent $250 just on the t-shirts

How about if ten of the t-shirts cost $20?

10 x $10 = $100

10 x $20 = $200

In this case, you would have spent $300 on t-shirts alone.

Add in three pairs of pants at $30 each. Now, you're up to $390.

Add in 10 pairs of shoes at $40 each. Now you're at $790. *This is just an incredibly small fraction of your entire wardrobe.* And you're probably not wearing half of these pieces either!

The dollar amount adds up fast doesn't it?

Now, look at the entirety of your closet. This includes tops, bottoms, shoes, handbags, coats, accessories, bed clothes, and undergarments. Chances are very good that you have spent more than twenty dollars on many pieces hanging in your closet. For example, blazers, sweaters, and blue jeans typically cost more than $20 even if they are deeply discounted or on clearance.

I'm not a fan of counting your clothes or restricting you to having a specific or limited number of clothes. However, it can be **a real eye-opener** to, just this once, count all the pieces in your wardrobe. To avoid tearing your closet apart, you can, at the very least, easily count the hanging pieces. Think about how much you spent on each piece. You can even be extremely conservative and low-ball the cost. Say you have 200 hanging pieces and you spent just five dollars on each piece. That's $1000 right there. But the reality is you've spent a lot more than five dollars on most of your pieces, like that leather jacket and that designer handbag. While you may be shocked at the sheer number of pieces you own and the amount of money you've spent, it's a wake-up call. When you realize you have 200 articles of clothing just on the hanging rack it can be startling. And when you admit you don't wear most of it this realization will help you to shop smarter.

You've probably heard the statistic that you wear 20% of your clothes 80% of the time. What do you think? Does this sound about right? If you want to see if these statistics are true for your wardrobe the formula to determine the percentage of items you actually wear is as follows:

Count the number of items worn divided by the number of items you have, then multiply by 100. This reveals the percentage of your wardrobe that you are and are not wearing.

For example: 25 items worn / 200 items total = 0.125 x 100 = 12.5% of your wardrobe is being worn and 87.5% of your wardrobe *is not* being worn

50 items worn / 200 items total = 0.25 x 100 = 25% of your wardrobe is being worn and 75% of your wardrobe *is not* being worn

Why does it matter

The purpose of this exercise is not to make you feel guilty or induce a panic attack! The purpose is, going forward, to help you make more thoughtful, smarter purchases. It's time to start treating your clothes and your closet like the major investment that they are. How will you make smarter purchases?

You will **no longer settle** for pieces that are "just okay" or "good enough."

You will **resist the impulse to buy** until you find the perfect pieces.

You will **acknowledge and then ignore** retailer's tactics to entice you to buy.

You will think **twice, and a third time**, before handing over your hard-earned money.

And you will **stop shopping so much**.

One way to estimate whether or not a potential purchase is worth the price is to use the **cost-per-wear formula**:

cost of item / number of times you anticipate wearing the piece each year = cost per wear. Some examples:

- wool blazer: cost $100 divided by 50 wearings comes to $2 per wearing

- floral print dress: cost $50 / 5 wearings = $10 per wearing

The cost-per-wear formula can also be used to evaluate the true of cost of clothes, shoes, and accessories that you have already purchased.

- Black jeans that you wear at least once a week: cost $50 / 52 wearings = 0.96

- Tan trench coat (that you bought because it was on a must-have list) cost $150 / 0 wearings = $150 down the drain!

Unworn pieces, like the trench coat, are the ones you really need to analyze to determine *why* you aren't wearing them. Unless they were a gift, you pulled out your wallet and willingly bought each top, bottom, and accessory in your closet. *Any pieces you are not wearing is not money well spent. It is wasted money.*

This brings us to a topic I briefly want to touch on, and that is the closet edit. Removing all the pieces that you never wear is an important component to getting a wardrobe that works for you. However, this is a major hurdle for many people. You protest that you can't just get rid of perfectly good pieces because you paid good money for them. But the key to moving forward is to remove these unworn pieces. The money is gone whether you are wearing them or not. If you want a reality check about how worthless most of your unworn clothes are try selling them online or have a yard sale. When no one wants your old jacket for a measly dollar, or even your unworn dress with the tags still attached for five dollars, the "value" hits home.

If you need more inspiration and advice on getting your closet organized and under control check out my other book: *An Imperfect Wardrobe*, and visit my blog Closetcures.com

Many of you may have already done a massive closet edit and were able to remove a lot of unworn pieces. That's great! You took a lot of time and put in a lot of effort to edit and organize your closet. It is categorized, colorized, and streamlined. But, you are still struggling to get dressed every day. You are frustrated and wonder what you are doing wrong...

So much emphasis is placed on purging your wardrobe, and rightly so, it's a vital part of the puzzle. However, editing your closet is not going to magically result in you loving your wardrobe. In fact, it might make you even more unhappy. You can clearly see what you are actually wearing and you might be less than thrilled.

This is why many people get discouraged. You are told to edit your closet to get a wardrobe you'll love. But after all that work you still struggle to get dressed. Because really, all a closet edit does is get rid of the stuff you are not wearing. And, again, this is an important part of having a well-functioning wardrobe. But, if you weren't that crazy about the clothes you do wear, you are still left with those same clothes. If you struggle to get dressed and are not happy with the results, the clothes you always wear are not working for you. Getting rid of unworn clothes does not solve this problem.

What is the solution? To shop smarter! This means making sure every new piece you add to your wardrobe is one you will wear.

In part one we talked about all the triggers and weaknesses that cause you to buy clothes you don't need, don't wear, and often don't even like that much. Now, it's time to learn how to be a savvy shopper. In part two we'll cover everything from raising your standards and shopping for your particular lifestyle, to why where and how you shop matters. In addition, we'll see why what you do after a shopping trip is so important. Finally, we'll ponder the benefits of a shopping slowdown.

To get started, we will talk about the five elements that you need to pay attention to in order to raise your standards. We'll identify what each of these elements means to you. Then, you can use this knowledge when shopping to know what to buy, what to avoid, and what to leave at the store. Because the key to keeping your wardrobe streamlined and under control is to not bring in any more pieces that you never wear.

PART II: SHOPPING SAVVY

Chapter 7

Raise Your Standards

STOP SETTLING FOR SUBPAR

I mage you had unlimited funds to shop for clothes. What would you buy? Would you head straight for the clearance rack and sale signs? Of course not! You would look at the pieces that appealed to you, make sure they fit, and you would buy them.

This is the same strategy you need to apply regardless of your budget. In fact, it is even more important to raise your standards when your funds are limited. You want to get the best quality and most versatile pieces to enhance your wardrobe. When you have quality pieces you love, you'll wear them more, and they'll last longer.

Does quality come with a higher price tag? Typically, yes.

Does this mean you can't buy as much? Typically, yes.

Here's the thing:

I understand the inner struggle to spend more than you are accustomed to on one or two pieces. It's scary. You think to yourself, "should I spend $125 on this one blazer when I could buy, like, 6 tops for the same price?" If it fits perfectly, is in your best shade, is something you want and need for your lifestyle, and you absolutely love it, then yes you should buy it. What good are 6 just okay tops that you rarely, if ever, wear? When you stop wasting money on "good deals" and clearance crap you will have the funds to buy better quality pieces. A closet filled with fewer, yet better, pieces suited just for you is how to curate a wardrobe you'll love.

How do you know if a shirt or a pair of pants is right for you? By making sure it meets your definition of the following five criteria:

1. Quality
2. Proper fit
3. Flattering shade
4. Lifestyle appropriate
5. Personal style

If just one of these five elements is off, you probably won't wear the piece. Let's look a little closer at each of these elements.

1. Quality

Although most of us do have limited wardrobe funds it is important to buy the best quality that you can reasonably afford. However, having limited funds is also a great reason to buy the best quality that you can reasonably afford. Choosing quality pieces is smart because your garments will look better, feel better, and last longer.

You might think you're saving money by buying the less expensive blazer, pair of shoes, or handbag. But poorly made clothes, in cheap, synthetic fabrics will quickly look worn, are more susceptible to rips and tears, and will need replaced sooner. And you might not wear them.

For example, you can buy three shirts made from a polyester blend for $15 each. Or you can buy one shirt made of 100% cotton that costs $45. Chances are you won't wear all three shirts because they look cheap and irritate your skin thanks to the polyester fabric. Whereas, if you buy the 100% cotton shirt that you really want for $45 dollars you can comfortably wear it while also looking better.

Keep in mind that investing in quality pieces does not mean you have to buy designer labels. There are lots of high quality brands that are lesser known. You just need to look at the details of each piece. The more you buy better quality pieces, the more you will appreciate that quality. You will no longer be willing to settle. How do you spot a quality piece? By paying attention to the two main factors that impact whether a piece is well made: fabric and construction.

Fabric

There are three types of fabric or fiber content: natural, synthetic, and blends. Synthetics are man-made, while natural fibers are, well, found in nature, and come from plants and animals. Synthetics are more affordable to make and cheaper to sell. However, they can be hot and clingy, whereas natural fibers are breathable. Blends are a combination of natural and synthetic fibers. Depending on the content distribution blends can be good or bad.

Synthetic fibers include:

- polyester – maintains shape and resists wrinkles, but is not breathable and can be hot to wear

- rayon - reduces static and pilling, and tends to drape well

- spandex - is lightweight and breathable, but is tight and clings

- microfibers - keeps out the cold, wind, and rain making it ideal for outerwear

Natural fibers include:
- cotton – soft and breathable

- silk – soft, luxurious, very durable and wicks away moisture; cool in summer and warm in winter.

- linen – breathable, strong, and lightweight, best for warm weather

- wool – very warm but some people find it itchy

Blends:

Blends can be the best of both worlds. For example, when synthetics are combined with natural fibers the garment will have fewer wrinkles, and will dry faster. Plus, they usually come with a lower price tag than one hundred percent natural fibers.

But beware. Even just a slight amount of certain synthetics can change the fit and care of a garment. Synthetics will shrink in a dryer that is too hot or when left in the dryer for too long. They are thinner making them more susceptible to rips and tears. And they are tighter and cling to the body potentially creating bulges. For example, a t-shirt that is 97% cotton, 3% spandex will cling to the body and potentially shrink in the dryer, whereas 100% cotton won't be as clingy or fragile. That little bit of spandex is all it takes.

I learned this the hard way when ordering t-shirts online. I thought I was ordering the exact same 100% cotton t-shirts as before. I loved the fit and wanted a few more colors. But when they arrived and I tried them on they were clinging to my mid-section and it was not flattering. I double-checked my order and sure enough these t-shirts had just a touch of spandex. To avoid the hassle and cost of returning them I thought, maybe I can wear them underneath sweaters or a blazer. But then I thought, what if I need to take off the blazer? I also tried a sweater over the t-shirt but the clinging was coming through the sweater. In other words, my stomach and side lumps were visible. I returned them.

Construction

Garment construction is evaluating how well the piece is made. To find out you must look at the following details:

- seams - do they lay flat, or are they bunching up; are they sewed (good) or glued (not as good)

- zippers - do they go up and down smoothly; is the zipper exposed or enclosed with fabric which protects the zipper and looks better

- pockets – do they lay flat, or are they creating extra bulk

- stitches – are they tight and flat, or are they uneven and not smooth

- buttons - are they tight and secure, or are they loose

- lining – higher quality pieces will have a lining; shirts with a back yoke or an extra panel between the shoulders are well constructed

- hems – should be finished with an extra panel rather than left loose and raw

- stiffer and heavier - the fabric has more heft and better coverage; lower quality garments can be sheer and flimsy

- good recovery - springs back to shape after being stretched or pulled which helps pieces to look better and last longer; lower quality will not recover easily

- prints and patterns - does the print or pattern match or lineup at the seams and points like the shoulder, collar, zipper, and buttons, or are prints and patterns uneven and mismatched

While color alone does not impact the quality, it can alter the *impression* of quality. With darker shades it is much harder to see poor garment construction.

Therefore, pay extra attention to the details on darker pieces in shades like black and navy blue.

Conduct an experiment. Compare two similar articles of clothing like a blazer. Choose a pricier piece to evaluate against a less expensive piece. Look for the construction points listed above. Notice the difference in the feel of each garment, look at the craftsmanship, the seams, and the lining. If you really want to go in depth with this experiment you can even buy both. See which blazer you prefer and actually wear. You can also ask a friend, housemate, or spouse which one they think is higher quality, looks better, and fits better. Don't reveal the price until they give a concrete answer. Just be sure to return the blazer you do not prefer.

2. Proper Fit

No matter what you choose to wear it should fit properly. Clothes should not be too tight or too baggy. Don't try to squeeze into clothes that are too tight because you don't like the size on the label. When clothes are too tight, they create bulges and are extremely uncomfortable. You may think bigger clothes will make you appear smaller. But they don't. Oversize clothes just look dowdy. Only buy and keep clothes that fit correctly.

When shopping for clothes wear neutral tops and bottoms that are easy to take on and off. Avoid wearing clothes with a bunch of buttons and zippers. Shoes should easily slip on and off. Make sure you are wearing you best, most supportive, undergarments in the shade of your skin tone. If you are shopping for a piece to go with something specific, such as a pair of work trousers, wear them or bring them along to see how they work with potential purchases.

Conduct an experiment. Pick a garment and take three sizes into the fitting room. Try on the size you think you are, a size larger, and a size smaller. Take note of how you look and feel in each size. Each brand has a fit model with different measurements which is why sizing is inconsistent from store to store. Do not let the number on the label discourage you from purchasing the size that fits you best.

3. Flattering Shade

You always hear the advice to wear your most flattering shades because it makes your eyes sparkle and your skin glow. When you wear shades that are less than ideal you can appear pale, tired, and rundown.

Many people are afraid it is too confusing trying to "find your best colors." I do agree that many methods are overwhelming because they try to get *too* detailed. Identifying your most flattering shades does not have to be as involved and confusing as it seems.

It is not about specific colors like blue, green, and red, because everyone can wear every color. Rather, ***it is about families of shades*** like cobalt blue vs. baby blue, pine green vs. olive green, and berry red vs. maroon red. To pinpoint your best shades think in terms of bright vs. muted, intense vs. soft, and warm vs. cool. Do you look best in jewel tones, soft pastels, icy tones, or earth tones?

Conduct an experiment. Compare two or more similar shades in natural lighting. See which looks best. For example, hold a few different shades of red next to your face. If you look at your face first it is a good shade for you. If you look at the garment first it is not your best shade. Typically, those who look better in a pure white shirt than an ecru or off-white shirt should stick to cool shades like soft pastels and icy tones. Conversely, those who look better in ecru or off-white should stick to warm shades like jewel tones and earth tones. Find your family of best shades and stick with them.

4. Lifestyle Appropriate

The clothes in your closet should be for the activities you do on a regular basis. Do not have clothes for your fantasy life, from your former career, or from when you were in college or high school. If you never go out for formal dinners or dancing don't keep multiple versions of these types of clothes. If you are retired, don't keep all your work clothes. Your clothes should also be weather appropriate. If the climate where you live is warm year-round there is no need to keep tons of winter clothes. Just have a few pieces on hand for the occasional cold day.

Conduct an experiment. Look through your closet and identify lifestyle areas that you have in abundance and those that are lacking. Do you have tons of jeans but no trousers? Do you have several heels but few flats? What do you find yourself needing for various situations? Which categories cause you the most stress because you never have what you need? These would be the categories you avoid when shopping. Make a list and a plan to purchase the missing pieces.

5. Personal Style

When you dress in clothes that match your personal style preferences you will feel confident and comfortable. But when you dress outside your personal style preferences you will feel like everyone is staring at you (and not in a good way). You will be eager to get out of those clothes.

If you work in a more formal business environment such as a law office but you have a laid-back style you may struggle to find clothes you like for work. The options may seem too formal and stiff.

Or, if you borrow a dress from your friend who dresses on the sexy side but you are more conservative you will feel uncomfortable the entire evening.

Conduct an experiment. Go to the mall and try on some pieces you normally avoid. For instance, if you hate floral prints try on a dress covered in flowers and see how you feel. Do you feel awkward and like everyone is staring at you? Then, try on the same or similar dress in a solid. How does it make you feel? Look at the clothes that are in the laundry each week because these are the clothes you are wearing. What do you like about them? Is it the fabric, the color, the neckline? What could you improve upon? By pinpointing your personal style preferences you will know which types of pieces you like and which to avoid.

These are the five elements that you need to be aware of to curate a wardrobe that works for you. Below are a few more things to keep in mind.

Make your own rules

Avoid standardized must-have lists. Everyone does not need, or want, a trench coat, a white button down blouse, a pencil skirt, and neutral heels. Create your own must-have list based your wardrobe woes, lifestyle needs, and personal preferences. If your style is laid-back and relaxed focus on high-quality, stylish anoraks or barn jackets. Get high-quality leather sandals and the best t-shirts you can find. Do not feel compelled to own a business suit or sexy dress if you'll never wear them.

Know yourself

Sometimes we want to buy things that we like but know from past experience that they don't work for our shape or our lifestyles. For me that would be button-up blouses. I like how they look on other people but not on me. Besides that, the buttons inevitably gap open.

Don't blame yourself when styles you like don't work for you. Every style will not work for every body type. Stick with what works for you. Stop trying to reinvent yourself on every shopping trip. This way of thinking stems from the influence of the fashion industry because they want your hard-earned money. There is nothing wrong with sticking with what you like. In fact, that is exactly what you should be doing if you want to love your wardrobe!

Don't settle

Clothes that are "just okay" can be the biggest challenge. Buying and wearing clothes that are "just okay" results in you feeling "just okay." They serve their purpose of decency, but do they serve the greater purpose of helping you to feel confident?

What makes a shirt "just okay" instead of an all star? You like it. Nothing is wrong with it. The fit, color, and style all work. But you just aren't excited about it. I want you to be excited to wear everything you buy. If you don't love it and are not excited by the prospect of wearing it then do not buy it.

Practice discipline

When shopping, it is important to be patient. This means taking the time to find things that actually work for you, that you like, that are in your best shades, and that fit properly. When you have trouble finding pieces that work do not settle and do not panic. It's okay to walk away without purchasing anything.

Raising your standards means making your own rules, setting your own priorities, and putting shopping systems in place that work for you. Avoid standardized must-have lists, know yourself, do not settle, and practice discipline.

Before you buy

When pondering a purchase or deciding whether or not to keep a piece make sure it passes your standards in regards to the five tests: quality, proper fit, flattering shades, lifestyle appropriate, and your personal style. Everything must work together. The perfect shade of blue does you no good if the sleeves are too short or the neckline is lower than you prefer. A perfectly fitting garment is great but not if it is a style you never wear or a shade that is less than flattering.

Be disciplined in your choices. Practice self-control. You don't want to keep adding items that will never be worn to your already overflowing closet.

Ask yourself if you really need another sweater?

Is this worthy of my wardrobe?

Is this shade flattering on my skin tone?

Do not lower your standards for a low price!

Be confident in your likes and dislikes and use them as your shopping guide. I want you to experience the joy of owning what you really, really want.

Would you rather spend $300 on more t-shirts, another pair of jeans, and yet another pair of shoes? Or, would you rather have one delicious, high-quality, buttery soft handbag that you look forward to using every single day?

Don't be surprised if once you raise your standards you find it harder and harder to find clothes, shoes, and accessories that you are willing to purchase.

Once you become accustomed to better quality pieces, the more you appreciate that quality. You will no longer be willing to settle. Instead, you will be motivated to keep looking until you find the best pieces for you.

It takes time to develop better shopping practices. Don't be so hard on yourself, but do be more thoughtful and present when clothes shopping.

You will still make some bad purchases...

You will still buy things you question once you get home...

And you will still have the occasional piece you thought you loved but never wear.

This is okay. Return what you should have left at the store as soon as you can and learn from your mistakes. Strive to do better next time.

We'll go into more detail later regarding reevaluating your purchases to determine whether or not you will wear them. In the meantime, let's talk about creating your customized shopping list, as well as go over various methods of allocating your wardrobe funds to ensure you get a wardrobe that works for you.

Chapter 8

Lifestyle Shopping

YOUR KEY TO SUCCESS

I t all ads up! A jacket here, a necklace there, and maybe another t-shirt or two since they are on sale. Before you know it, you've spent a lot of money on pieces that you will stick in your already stuffed closet possibly to never even be worn.

As we've discussed, it's all too easy to get caught up in the excitement of shopping causing us to lose focus. That's why an important part of a smart clothes shopping strategy is having a detailed shopping list which includes a budget. Establishing a budget and creating a detailed shopping list lets you see exactly how much money you have, how much you are spending, and what you are spending it on. Think of your budget as investing in yourself. You want to make smart choices. The value of a well-planned clothing budget and list is that it keeps you on track forcing you to make strategic decisions based on your wardrobe goals, rather than on emotional triggers. Without a budget or predetermined spending limit you risk spending more than you realize on impulse buys and clothes you'll never wear.

Keeping an eye on your finances is the key to keeping your wardrobe in working order and under control. When you have a budget pieces start to add up quickly and your remaining budget gets smaller and smaller. Your dwindling dollars prompt you to think twice about whether you want to spend your hard-earned clothing budget on each potential purchase. With that being said, a budget can take the guilt out of spending as long as you are paying cash, you want and need it, and it's on your shopping list. You have this money allocated for clothes, so shopping can be fun!

In this chapter you'll learn:

- how to set a shopping budget

- how to make a prioritized shopping list

- how to know if a high price is worth it

- if it ever make sense to shop the clearance racks

- if it is ever okay to make an unplanned purchase

Let's dig in!

Create your shopping budget

The first step in creating your shopping budget is to determine how much money you have to spend on clothes. Set your yearly amount based on 5% of your take-home pay. Feel free to increase or decrease as you see fit, but this is the most common recommendation. For example, if you bring home $50,000 annually multiply that by 5% and you get $2,500 per year to spend on clothes, shoes, and accessories.

Now, I do not advise spending the whole amount in one or two huge shopping expeditions. What I do recommend is a slow and steady approach to shopping.

Why?

Needs and wants shift over time. You might take up a new hobby. Perhaps your favorite coat gets a giant hole and needs replaced immediately. Sometimes you can't find everything you need on one shopping trip. Maybe you don't like the selections and prefer to wait for new merchandise to arrive in stock. Sometimes, you inadvertently overlook a need while making your shopping list. You forgot that your sneakers were looking ratty until you wore them to the grocery store. Or, you realize you could use a lightweight shirt jacket to wear in air conditioning after spending a miserable day freezing at work.

Once you have determined your total yearly budget choose how to divvy up your dollars by breaking it down into spending buckets. There are many different methods you can use. Pick the one that makes the most sense for you.

Using the $2,500 example from above you can allocate:

- half ($1,250) for warm weather, half ($1,250) for cold weather

- 1/4 ($625) per season or every three months: Spring, Summer, Fall, Winter

- a percentage for each category: shoes, coats, tops, bottoms, accessories, undergarments, bed clothes, workout clothes

- a higher percentage for needs, a lower percentage for wants

- a higher dollar amount for big ticket items like winter coat, boots, and handbags

- a smaller percentage for trendy pieces

- half for work, half for leisure

What if your take home pay is $30,000? That gives you $1,500 per year to spend on clothes, shoes, and accessories. You might choose:

- half ($750) for warm weather, half ($750) for cold

- 1/4 ($375) per season or every three months: Spring, Summer, Fall, Winter

- $1,000 for work clothes, $500 for leisure wear

Make your prioritized shopping list

Once you determine your budget the next step is to work on your shopping list. This entails writing down all the clothes, shoes, and accessories that you want and need. Then, rank them in order of most important or most needed, to least important or not urgently needed.

Be ask specific as possible when making your list. Think about the categories where you struggle the most when getting ready. The goal is a fully functioning, versatile wardrobe filled with mix and match pieces in your best shades that suit your personal style preferences. You want to get dressed without the stress. The goal should not be an entirely new wardrobe every year. When the majority of your clothes are well-made, high quality pieces they should last for several years. The idea is to refresh your wardrobe each season with just a few key pieces, and to replace or update well-loved items that are starting to show wear.

The pieces you hate shopping for are typically the most underrepresented in your wardrobe. Consequently, the absence of these pieces are a major cause of your struggles when dressing. When you think about your wardrobe and getting dressed which categories are always a struggle?

Do you never seem to have the right shoes to wear with your trousers?

Do you find yourself wishing you had some dressier shirts that are not cotton t-shirts?

Do you want to focus on pants, or are you in need of some jackets?

You should also be thinking about want you want from your wardrobe. What do you want to add, or how do you want to steer it? Do you want to add more patterns, or infuse it with a new color? Would you like some comfortable pieces to wear around the house that are also flattering and fit well? Maybe you want to get some more daring pieces for nights out?

Disperse your dollars

Using your predetermined wardrobe budget allocate funds to each piece based on your prioritized list. This is where you estimate how much each article of clothing might cost and how much you are willing to pay for it. While not an exact science since you can't know prices ahead of time, you can anticipate how much each piece will cost, as well as how much you are willing to spend on different things.

To track your purchases and ensure you remain in budget write down every purchase, the price, where you bought it, and why you bought it or the activities for which you plan to wear it. You can use a spending app or simply keep an actual list, whatever works for you. Start with the budgeted amount and deduct each purchase as you go. This way, you can easily see how much you've spent, as well as how much you have left. Be sure to note whether it was full price, on sale, markdown, or clearance. All of this helps you to see if you are shopping smart or thoughtlessly.

Let's use the $2500 yearly wardrobe budget as our example and split it in half for warm weather and cold weather. This gives you a healthy $1250 to allocate for each. You can get a lot for that money, as well as invest a little bit more on higher quality pieces. Below is an example of purchases, the cost, and the dwindling budget for warm weather.

Warm weather purchases with a $1250 budget:

- slip on leather sandals: $100 ($1150)

- three pairs of shorts for $30 each: $90 ($1060)

- a lightweight rain jacket: $125 ($935)

- a swimsuit: $75 ($860)

- four tank tops for $20 each: $80 ($780)

These were your needed and planned for purchases.

Midway through the season you realize you need a few things that are not on your original list. These are pieces you completely forgot about or overlooked until the need arose. As you are thinking about what to take to the beach for your upcoming vacation you remember you wanted a cover-up for your swimsuit and some flip flops for walking on the sand. You also want to get a lightweight cross body bag for walking along the boardwalk.

Remember the grubby sneakers you didn't think about needing replaced until you wore them out in public? You also want a gold tone pair of sunglasses to wear with the gold tone jewelry you got for your birthday. And you want to find a lightweight shirt jacket to layer over tank tops.

- white swimsuit cover up: $25 ($755)

- silver flip flops: $35 ($720)

- lightweight cross body bag: $125 (595)

- navy sneakers: $40 ($555)

- gold tone sunglasses: $20 ($532)

- lightweight shirt jacket: $40 ($495)

As for completely unplanned for purchases, you did buy two items. Your favorite brand has your favorite lightweight cotton sweatshirt in a new tomato red color. And you spot a pair of sneakers in the same tomato red shade and in your preferred sneaker brand. These are wardrobe staples in updated colors that you will definitely wear.

- tomato red lightweight sweatshirt: $45 ($450)

- tomato red sneakers: $40 ($410)

As the season ends you may find you didn't spend the total allotted amount. That's fine. You can either roll it over into next season's budget, use it on something besides clothes, or save it. Do not feel compelled to try to spend it all just for the sake of spending it. Just because you have $410 left that doesn't mean you should raid the clearance racks and hit up the discount stores in order to get a large haul of merchandise.

While your list is your guide, it's not set in stone. As wants and needs change, such as switching jobs or taking up a hobby, adjust your list accordingly. And as you shop for pieces and try them on you might come to the realization that you just don't like cardigans despite putting them on your list. After trying on every size and shade of cardigan available you realized structured blazers and shirt jackets are more your style.

Be somewhat flexible. For instance, if you're having trouble finding a black one-button linen blazer but you find a navy two-button cotton blazer that fits perfectly you might want to get it. On the other hand, do not splurge on a bright purple double-breasted silk blazer when you're looking for a neutral investment piece. You do not want a closet filled with random pieces that don't go together, nor in shades that are not flattering. A low price and lots of options do you no good if you never wear them.

While you may think you want a sparkly silver dress to wear for formal occasions the reality is you never attend any. Besides, you look better in gold.

You may see a pair of three-inch high bright red pumps and envision yourself wearing them out on a date. However, you really hate wearing heels and you are not into the dating scene.

And while it might be nice to have another pair of boots, the truth is you already have six pairs, yet you always wear the same two pairs. You don't need any more boots and you should get rid of the four pairs you never wear.

Be very conscious not to go over your budget. If you do, chances are good that you're making a lot of impulse purchases. While not all impulse purchases are bad, the majority go unworn. If you find yourself close to exceeding your predetermined budget early in the season reevaluate what you have bought thus far. Did you cave to a wardrobe weakness or the lure of a low price? Do you love it all and need it all? Or, should you return a few pieces?

Perhaps you don't want to spend 5% of your income on your wardrobe because you have a goal to pay down debt, or to buy a house or a new car, yet you still want to look good. What should you do?

This goes back to priorities and most urgent needs, as well as versatility. Sometimes all it takes is a few key pieces to jazz up your wardrobe. Pump up an existing t-shirt and jeans wardrobe by adding a cool blazer and some fresh shoes. Throw on a statement necklace and it's a whole new outfit.

To get the most from your budget focus on all-season wardrobe work-horses that can either be worn alone or layered for the majority of the year. Layering pieces are essential for those cold mornings that turn into warm, if not hot, afternoons, and then cool down again as evening approaches. This is where the bulk of your budget should go to get the maximum mileage out of your wardrobe and your dollars. These pieces will be worn often because they are versatile and flexible. Stick with one or two neutrals and a few core colors in your best shades. Add one or two prints for interest. Plaids and stripes are always good print choices. Look for neutral, timeless styles and cuts rather than extreme designs. Resist buying multiples when one will do. It is tempting to purchase something you like in multiple colors, but do you really need them?

Only buy what you truly need. The average person needs clothes for activities like running errands, carting kids around, work clothes for an increasingly casual world, trips to the mall, and lounging around the house. Most people do not need several options for formal events. They just don't. Be honest about your real life. Do not assemble a wardrobe for your fantasy life, or the life of a friend or relative.

If you are really afraid you won't have anything for a spur of the moment, last minute invite to a wedding, fancy cocktail party, or work event, then get just one outfit for such occasions. If you wear the piece once in one year you will be lucky.

Is it worth the price to me

There's always the question: "Would I pay full price for this?"

And we're always told if the answer is no then leave it at the store. However, this is not always the best barometer. There's a difference between buying something *just because it's a good deal* and buying something you like *that also happens to be a good deal*.

A graphic t-shirt might be on sale for $9.99 with a regular price of $25. Would you pay $25 bucks for it? Probably not. But you really do love it and it's only $9.99, so you should buy it. You might really like that t-shirt but at $25 it would be out of your budget. However, it fits into your budget nicely at $9.99.

Your mind might play tricks on you. Since it's marked down or on clearance you know it will never be a possibility that you would have to spend full price. Therefore, you might tell yourself that you *would* pay full price. But, the reality is you would not.

A better question is: "Is it worth the price to me?" This is the question you should be asking when pondering any potential purchase regardless of whether it is full price, half off, or on the clearance rack. To come to an answer it must meet the five high standards we discussed in the previous chapter: quality, proper fit, flattering shade, lifestyle appropriate, and your personal style. In addition, it should also pass the cost-per-wear test. Divide the price tag by the number of times you anticipate wearing it to get the cost per wear.

Many of us think, "I could never spend $150 for a pair of jeans" (even though they fit like a glove, you love them, and you expect to wear them several times a week). But you don't hesitate to spend $150 on a bunch of junk from the clearance racks. If you wear the $150 jeans twice each week for $52 weeks that comes out to a cost of $1.44 per wear. That's a much better use of your money than spending $150 on various clearance items that you'll be lucky if you wear more than once, if at all.

Clothing prices are based on many factors. At the most basic level, the goal for manufactures and retailers, first and foremost, is to make a profit. To do so they must factor in garment construction costs including labor, materials, and shipping. For example, wallets may be small but they have many intricate little details that increase the price tag.

There is also the perceived value of a brand that sets the bar for how much you are willing to pay. Companies choose how much to invest in marketing. Do they want to hire a famous actress or model to feature in expensive tv and print ads? This helps elevate the perceived value of the brand status so they can charge more. Consumers are willing to pay more for brands that put them in an exclusive club.

One method to help you decide is to use the cost-per-wear formula we discussed in the *Down the Drain* chapter. Again, not an exact science as you can't know for sure how many times you will wear a garment. But you can make an educated guess. The number of times you anticipate wearing a garment should be high to justify the purchase, regardless of the price.

Some clothes can be worn year-round while others are specific to extremely hot or cold weather. While you won't be wearing your pricey leather sandals in the middle of winter you will probably wear them several times a week, if not every single day, throughout the summer. The same goes for a quality winter coat.

Each season you will likely have a few big ticket items that take up a large chunk of your wardrobe budget such as a designer handbag, three-quarter length wool coat, and a cashmere sweater. These are your wardrobe workhorses, therefore, they are the ones that you should invest in. You should have them for years to come, you should wear them often, and they should be a high quality that will stand up to frequent use.

It's also a good idea to identify types of clothes and features that you do not like. Make a list of all the things you can think of that have annoyed you in the past. While you cannot foresee all annoyances it will help you catch a lot before committing to a purchase. Being aware is the key. Knowing what you do and do not like based on past issues is helpful in avoiding bad purchases. Below are just a few of my pet peeves:

- shoes with laces - I hate when they come untied and I hate fussing with them

- high heels - I find them beyond uncomfortable and unnatural

- shoes that rub against my heel - I avoid sandals with back straps

- button up shirts - because they always gap across the chest

- shirts that are too low cut - I am self-conscious and simply avoid them

- leggings - I prefer to not have fabric clinging to my large hips and thighs

- turtlenecks – I don't like anything tight around my neck

It's important to note that not everything is for everyone and not everything will work with every body type. Identify the pieces you like but know you don't feel confident wearing. Don't keep buying these things in the hopes that one day you will suddenly love how they look on you. There are lots of things I wish I could wear but never feel confident and comfortable in once they are on. For example, I have accepted that I will never like the look of a belt or scarf on me. I love them on other people, but not on me. I really love the look of slouchy pants with a belt. But pants are always tight on my large thighs. They are never slouchy or loose. This is why I also avoid leggings and skinny jeans with cute boots. I envy those who can wear these looks.

Does it ever make sense to shop the clearance racks?

In my opinion, no. Everything on the clearance rack is something that no one wanted all season. The entire section is based on a deeply discounted price.

Is it ever okay to make an unplanned purchase?

Of course, as long as it meets your personal criteria. Although unplanned purchases cut into your wardrobe budget, sometimes it's worth it! You want to enjoy your wardrobe. As long as it's not a common occurrence it is just fine to make the occasional unplanned purchase.

Shopping doesn't have to be all drudgery or hard work. It can be lots of fun. As long as you mainly stick to the pieces on your wants and needs list, buy good quality garments, and stay within your budget you can shop without regret.

Now that you've identified your shopping weaknesses and buying triggers, faced up to the fact that you've wasted a lot of money on unworn clothes over the years, understand the importance of raising your standards, and created a budget and a list, it's time to go shopping!

Chapter 9

Location, Location, Location

MAKE GOOD USE OF YOUR TIME

T he average size of a shopping mall is approximately 164,000 square feet with around 100 stores, and a food court with about 8 restaurants. A typical shopper spends at least two hours at the mall. When people travel to a destination mall they tend to be there all day. Since they don't visit often they want to make it worth the drive. Plus, they will inevitably stumble upon some stores they have never been in before.

Grove City Outlets, which is a destination mall in Pennsylvania, has 120 - 130 stores. Bus loads of people visit every day from all over the United States and Canada. If you were to visit all 120 stores and spend just 5 minutes in each store it would take you over 8 hours! Of course, you won't go in every single store. A woman shopping for herself won't go into the men's stores or the children's stores, nor will she patronize every restaurant at the food court. If she's not in the market for fine jewelry she will breeze past the jewelry stores. Unless she needs shoes, she may skip those stores too. That still leaves at least 50 women's clothing stores.

Now, she will be faced with some choices. There are several stores she knows she doesn't like so she can skip those. Sometimes she ventures into stores she has not visited before, so she may take a peak and quickly walk through them. However, there will probably be around 10 stores she knows, likes, and will spend more than 5 minutes in, checking out the merchandise, trying things on, and making purchases. Since these stores are spread throughout the entire mall, rather than right next to each other, it takes time to walk to each one.

Once inside a store you are not looking at every single rack and every piece of clothing. There is no way possible thanks to the abundance of merchandise. You are constantly forced to make snap judgments about which racks to look at and which ones probably aren't for you. After repeating this process in a few stores many people start to get frustrated, lose interest, and get tired, thirsty, and hungry. It's a perfect time for a break. Unfortunately, the food court is, you guessed it, at the other end of the mall.

What if you tried to look at every single rack, in every single store to ensure you aren't missing the perfect piece? How about every rack in just one store? This is highly unrealistic. But, if you could what do you think would be the result? How many pieces out of the entire mall would work for you, your lifestyle, and your personal style? My guess is not many.

You might be thinking it's easier to shop online. You don't have to waste time driving to the store, finding a parking spot, dodging pushy salespeople, and trekking all over the mall juggling shopping bags. From the comfort of your couch you can shop twenty-four hours a day. You can walk away from the computer for a while and come back later to see if you still want those items in your cart. There are more colors and sizes available than in the typical brick-and-mortar store. You can customize your search criteria, add items to your cart, edit it later, and read reviews. And you can easily compare several brands and options at once.

However, online shopping comes with a different set of challenges. You can't touch, examine, or try on the garments. The color in the picture may look different in person. You have to wait for the items to be delivered. And, returns are a hassle and an extra expense.

Today, many retailers have both brick-and-mortar stores and a website. This is called omnichannel retailing. It at all works together providing more options for shoppers. Since there are pros and cons to both in person and online shopping many people do a combination of both. This has lead to the creation of three new words or phrases: showrooming, webrooming, and bracketing.

Showrooming is the act of visiting a physical store so you can touch, feel, and try on items. But, you make your purchases online.

Webrooming is the opposite. You pre-shop online, and then visit the brick and mortar store to make your purchases.

Bracketing is when you buy multiple sizes, colors, or slight variations of an item, try them on at home, and return the ones you don't want. It makes sense that people do this for online purchasing, but people also do it with items they bought at a brick-and-mortar store. Why? Perhaps you want to see how they look with your other clothes, maybe you were in a hurry or didn't feel like trying the pieces on, or maybe you simply despise the fitting rooms.

As we've discussed frequently throughout this book there is an abundance of choices when it comes to shopping. That also includes making decisions about the type of store to visit. Stores vary in size, square feet, layout, price points, and assortment of merchandise. You can choose a department store, specialty store, fast-fashion store, off-price store, or a big box discount store.

There are benefits and drawbacks associated with different types of stores. While there are no right or wrong places to shop, where you choose to shop for the majority of your clothes does matter and impacts your wardrobe when it comes to such things as coordination of styles, colors, and the level of quality. We choose which stores to visit or websites to patronize based on the company attributes or their image. These attributes include price level, types of promotions, product assortment, quality, service, and convenience. Being aware of the types of merchandise, their specialization, and target customer can help you make the best use of your time.

Let's look a little closer at the various types of stores and how they might impact your wardrobe.

Department Stores

The average department store is around 250,000 square feet and often uses the loop layout to connect customers to every department. There are high-end department stores (Bloomingdales, Nordstrom, Lord & Taylor, Neiman Marcus), mid-priced department stores (Macy's), and lower priced discount department stores (JCPenny, Kohl's).

Department stores sell a mix of well-known brands, as well as in-house brands that are created for, and sold exclusively at, the department store. They have a wide and deep assortment, in a broad range of price points, categories, and styles. Basically, there is something for everyone.

Department stores have well-planned layouts and create floor plans that merchandisers follow. The stores are laid out in small "shops" or sections for each brand, designer, and category to help the shopper take the guesswork out of creating outfits. Each section contains clothes that are similar in style, color, and quality.

Some shoppers avoid department stores because they are too big. It takes a lot of time to walk through the store. Many people think the prices are too high at more upscale department stores, like Bloomingdales, while others view the merchandise at JCPenny as lower quality and less stylish.

How shopping at department stores impacts your wardrobe

If the majority of your clothes come from department stores, you probably have a well-rounded wardrobe, depending on how you shop while in the store. If you stick to just one or two designers most of your pieces will coordinate well together. However, buying clothes from all over the store can result in some random purchases. Pick a few designers that make clothes that work for your budget, lifestyle, body type, and personal style preferences. Shop those first and do the bulk of your shopping there. Then, venture into some of the other departments once in a while to add a few pieces for interest and personality.

Off-Price Retailers

Discount retailers, also known as off-price department stores, include companies like Marshall's, Gabe's, Burlington, and Ross Dress For Less. Stores can range in size from approximately 30,000 square feet, like TJMaxx, to upwards of 120,000 square feet like Nordstrom Rack. Their business model is to take all the leftover inventory and cast offs from other companies that did not sell resulting in a wide range of brands and categories. There is no planning or coordination of colors, brands, or styles. By the time this merchandise gets to discount retailers it is from the previous season.

The store buys in bulk and stuffs everything onto large racks. The only distinctions they make in merchandising the store are for size and type of garment like tops, bottoms, or coats. Otherwise, it's a free-for-all. That's why their stores look like one giant clearance section or a garage sale. And if you choose to do the majority of your shopping at discount retailers your closet will look like their stores: a sea of mismatched colors, patterns, styles, and cheap fabrics.

While some people love the thrill of the hunt, that, unfortunately, is what turns your closet into a mass of clothes you don't like and never wear. I realize that many people shop at discount stores because they are on a budget and have limited funds to spend on their wardrobes. But those seemingly inexpensive purchases add up. And, you often end up spending more without even realizing it because the prices are so low.

How shopping at off-price stores impacts your wardrobe

The main advantage of shopping at discount stores is the low prices. This is great if you find something you need, in your style and color, that fits perfectly, and coordinates with your existing wardrobe.

However, you can easily overspend when you buy based mainly on a low price. If the majority of your wardrobe comes from discount stores you will struggle to put together outfits because most of the clothes they sell there are from previous seasons and different brands. They are the pieces no one wanted at other stores. Plus, discount stores don't sell a lot of basic, staple items which are what ground your outfits. Instead, they tend to have leftover trendy pieces that quickly look dated.

For those of you who really enjoy hunting for bargains at discount stores try to limit your visits, go with a pre-determined budget for how much you can spend, and don't exceed it. Think carefully before committing to any purchase. Pay attention to the fabric and construction of each garment.

Specialty Apparel Stores

When a store is on the smaller side and only sells apparel, jewelry, and possibly shoes, it's referred to as a boutique. The majority of stores in traditional shopping malls and outlet malls are small boutique-type stores. Unlike department and off-price stores that sell everything from housewares to toys, specialty apparel stores focus on selling apparel. Their retail mix is narrow and deep with a highly defined, yet limited, selection of clothes, shoes, and accessories. Usually, they only sell their own brand of merchandise.

Every boutique has a certain vibe. There are high-end designer boutiques (Michael Kors), less-expensive boutiques (Old Navy) and everything in between (J. Crew). Some are more formal and cater to clothes for work, like Talbots, while others are more casual and rugged, like L.L. Bean. They might also have a vertical retail model specializing in one category, such as athleisure, as Lululemon does.

The average size of a specialty store will vary greatly. For instance, J.Crew is typically about 2,000 square feet, compared with Old Navy which is around 15,000 square feet. However, their is no size limit. The store layout can be free flow to prompt curiosity, or a loop, grid, or diagonal layout.

How shopping at boutiques impacts your wardrobe

Shopping trips are more efficient when sticking to boutiques that work for you. You can save yourself a lot of time by visiting boutiques that offer the types of clothing you need and prefer for your lifestyle. When you buy clothes at boutiques that don't match your personal style you probably won't ever wear the clothes.

The are several benefits to repeatedly shopping at the same few boutiques. Mainly, the fit is consistent because they use the same type of fit model to cut the clothes. Another benefit is when you buy several items from one brand you will have a cohesive look because the shades and styles were designed to work together as part of that collection. Everything works together in season, and flows well into the next and upcoming seasons. The shades and styles are often consistent from season to season, therefore, clothes from previous seasons should coordinate well with new pieces.

However, buying your entire wardrobe from just one boutique or designer can make you look like a walking billboard for the company. It can also stifle your creativity and cause you to quickly tire of your wardrobe.

Fast-Fashion Stores

The newest category of retailer is fast fashion stores like H&M, Zara, and Topshop. Their business model is to sell a wide range of trendy, affordable clothes that appeal to a lot of people. They sell rapidly constructed knockoffs inspired by high fashion pieces making them a cheaper version of the high-end boutiques.

How shopping at fast-fashion stores impacts your wardrobe

There are not a lot of basics at fast-fashion stores. Instead, you will find current trends that look dated after just one season. The price point is low because the quality is low, the fabric is mostly synthetic, and the style is only in for a limited time. That's why these business models are quickly getting a bad reputation. Many refer to it as disposable fashion since it is only wearable for a season or two. When your closet is filled with fast fashion pieces this leads to frustration with your wardrobe. The ultimate result is a lot of clothes in landfills.

Big Box Discount Stores

Walmart and Target are a combination or hybrid model of the department store and off-price stores. They have current merchandise and permanently low prices. Typically, they serve as the anchors for strip malls. Big box stores can range in size from 50,000 square feet up to 200,000 square feet. They use the grid or loop layout.

How shopping at big box discount stores impacts your wardrobe

While Walmart is not known for its fashionable clothes, Target has gained a reputation for stylish pieces at affordable prices. Several high fashion designers have created low price lines that are featured in Target. You can find some good pieces at a good price at big box stores, just be aware that the quality is not always the best.

Brick-and-Mortar Shopping Tips

- plan your route - check out the layout, store directory, and entrances

- pre-shop the store websites - take note of styles, shades, and price points

- fitting room - take several sizes so you don't have to keep getting dressed and undressed

- avoid your weaknesses - if you can't resist a bargain steer clear of the clearance racks

- take notes - write down details and the price of potential purchases so you don't forget later in the day

- take breaks - have a snack or a beverage, think about what you've seen thus far

- know your budget - determine how much you can afford to spend and are willing to spend

- shop on weekdays - stores are more organized, less crowded, and fully stocked

Online Shopping Tips

- pay attention to the details - fabric content (even a slight bit of synthetic can impact fit as well as thickness or thinness of a garment), where the hem lands (mid-hip or at waist), the fit (slim, classic, or relaxed); when in doubt about size go up not down, too big is better than too small and tight

- pictures - zoom in, look at every picture, look at different colors (even if you want a black shirt look at it in white or a lighter color so you can see the subtle details which can be difficult to see on a black shirt in a picture)

- shades - garment colors can look different in pictures than what it looks like in person

- the model - note her body shape (sometimes they give her actual measurements), if yours is not similar think about how the clothes might look on you

- reviews - some companies show the height, weight, and shape of the reviewer which is beneficial for selecting a size; you gain insight into whether it runs big, small, or is true to size; positive and negative reviews tend to give the most detail, look for patterns such as super soft or scratchy fabric

- shipping costs - what are they

- return policy and or fees - what are they, do they have a brick and mortar store where you can return items

- buy just one top and one bottom - see how it works out and how the brand fits before ordering a lot of pieces in several colors

Where you choose to shop impacts the state of your wardrobe and the ease with which you get dressed. Whether in person or online the vibe of the retailer has to be similar to your personal style preferences and lifestyle needs. Remember, each company has a brand story. For the most cohesive wardrobe, stick to just a few stores for the majority of your purchases, and sprinkle in some pieces from other retailers to add interest and variety. Now, I'm not saying that you must only buy one brand of clothes, or that you should never shop at discounters. In fact, mixing brands and price points, while adding your own touches are what give you your unique personal style. But you do need some semblance of order with your wardrobe.

If you work from home or have a job where you can wear jeans and a t-shirt to work you will have little need for the business clothes sold at Ann Taylor.

If you're in the market for outdoor clothing for hiking or camping your first choice should not be Macy's or Chico's. Don't make things harder than they have to be. Instead, shop at The North Face, REI Co-op, Land's End, Eddie Bauer, Patagonia, or Duluth Trading Company.

Regardless of where you shop for clothes make sure everything you buy works for your lifestyle needs, your personal style, fits properly, is in your best shades, and that the quality matches the price tag. These are the keys to loving your clothes. And that is how you stop buying clothes you never wear.

In the next chapter we'll discuss what to do when you get home with your new purchases to ensure you made smart choices.

Chapter 10

Love or Lust

REVIEWING YOUR PURCHASES

W hen you get home and put away your purchases you should be excited
about what you bought and eager to wear everything. The new clothes,
shoes, and accessories should work well with your existing wardrobe and look

like they belong in your closet. You should be okay with what you paid and what you got for your money.

Unfortunately, this is not always the case.

As with all things related to our wardrobes, post purchase evaluations are charged with emotions. Returning home from a shopping trip can be depressing. It can be a let-down. The high of shopping is gone and you begin to experience post purchase anxiety and buyer's remorse. This is also known as post purchase cognitive dissonance, which is a fancy term for the negative emotions and unhappiness you experience after making a purchase. Some post purchase emotions might include shame, anxiety, stress, embarrassment, regret, and disappointment with yourself for wasting money on a bunch of stuff that you suspect you'll never wear. In other words, buyer's remorse.

Now that you are back to the reality of your closet you need to reevaluate each purchase to be sure it meets your new high standards. Ensuring you truly love your new purchases is the key to wearing the clothes in your wardrobe, to not re-cluttering your closet, and to spending your money wisely. Post purchase evaluation is a crucial step in your purchasing journey because it directly impacts the state of your wardrobe. This is when you gauge whether you are excited to wear the clothes or secretly wish you had left them at the store. This is when you decide whether you will keep your purchases or if you should return them.

When you question why you bought an article of clothing your natural inclination is to defend your purchase (even if it is defending it to yourself). You engage in post purchase rationalization where you try to talk yourself into liking the items you bought. Although you tell yourself this was a wise purchase, there's a battle going on in your head about whether or not you should have bought it. Basically, you are taking both sides of the argument.

What are some thoughts, emotions, or situations that might trigger buyer's remorse:

- you don't need it - it was an unplanned purchase, it was frivolous, you already have several colors and versions

- you went overboard - you bought way too much

- you overspent - you charged it instead of paying cash, went over budget

- passing on pieces - you wish you would have gotten something else, or a different color or style

- unrealistic expectations - the product does not meet your expectations be they realistic or unrealistic

- you were settling - because you couldn't find what you really wanted, or you didn't want to spend the money

- wardrobe orphans - they don't work with the rest of your wardrobe

- it seemed good at first - but then you don't wear it, or immediately want to take it off when you do

We've talked about most of these issues throughout this book. Now, let's look at each of them in relation to post-purchase evaluation.

You Don't Need It

What about when you don't need a piece but you really, really want it? This is known as variety seeking buying behavior. It tends to kick in when you grow bored with your wardrobe so you go shopping. You don't *need* anything, you just *want* something fresh. Sometimes, we get the itch to buy something new in a different color or style than usual. There is nothing wrong with this, in moderation. The occasional fun shopping trip for a few relatively inexpensive pieces to breath new life into your wardrobe is fine. We all need a special treat once in a while.

While there is nothing wrong with trying a different style make sure it works for you before cutting off the tags. Again, as long as it meets your high standards and you know you will wear it go ahead and keep it. Just don't make it a habit. Too much unstructured, unplanned purchasing results in adding pieces to your wardrobe that you quickly tire of and don't wear because they aren't right for you, and don't serve your lifestyle needs. These purchase just clog up your closet.

If it was an impulse piece that you bought due to a low price tag, or for activities you never do, then you should return it as soon as possible.

You Went Overboard

When you buy things you don't need or things you didn't set out to purchase you end up with a packed, disjointed closet. It's easy to get caught up in the excitement of shopping. All the new styles and beautiful colors are enticing causing you to fall prey to shiny object syndrome. Everything looks good and you get seduced by the low prices causing all logic to go out the window. Perhaps you caved into one of your wardrobe weaknesses, like I often do with t-shirts.

What can you do when you realize you went overboard?

When you buy more than you set out to, or bought pieces you don't really need, think about whether or not you will wear them. Be honest. If so, keep them. If not, return them.

You Overspent

Despite the best of intentions sometimes you do overspend. This is likely to happen when you go overboard with your purchases and cave to impulse buys. If you spent more than you had budgeted for a piece or bought something that wasn't on your shopping list the crucial questions are:

- Do you really love it, need it, want it, and are excited to wear it?

- Is it flattering and does it fit properly?

- Does it go with your other clothes?

- Is it your personal style?

• Will you wear it enough that the cost-per-wear will be low?

If the answers are all yes then I would keep it. Sometimes we find something that is our version of perfection and that makes it worth the higher price tag. However, if the answers are a resounding *no* return it as soon as possible.

Passing On Pieces

There is post purchase regret about what you bought, but there is also post purchase regret about what you left at the store. It's inevitable that there will be all kinds of clothes, shoes, and accessories that you regret not buying. It happens all the time.

You bought the blue blouse but wish you would have bought the red one...

You got a skirt off the clearance rack when the one you fell in love with (and left at the store) was full price...

Passing on pieces makes smart shopping sense since you don't have an unlimited budget. However, it does not mean you won't have regrets. This is known as post-purchase dissonance. The reason you're rethinking your purchases is because you're ruminating about all the alternatives you left at the store. The mental toll of it weighs on you.

If there was something you just can't stop thinking about you may want to go back and just get it. If you love the blue blouse and plan on wearing it a lot, go ahead and get the red one too.

If you can return the clearance piece, do so, and get the one you really wanted.

Dissonance also occurs when you regret buying something because you think you could have found something even better. Despite really liking your purchase you wonder what you could have bought instead. You wonder if you could have found a better price or more color options if you had just kept looking.

How do you prevent, reduce, or avoid post-purchase dissonance? Realize there will always be something better, less expensive, and new out there. At some point you must be all in on your current purchase. Just because there are other options that does not belittle your purchase.

Unrealistic Expectations

Post-purchase evaluation entails comparing your purchase with the expectations you had when you bought it. When you are in one mindset or mood at
the store, and another after returning home, it can cause regret. This goes back
to the question of *what were you really shopping for?* If you were shopping for
reasons other than to purchase needed clothes, you may well experience post
purchase regret.

Your desire for something overshadowed or overpowered your rational side.
In the heat of the moment, when you are experiencing the high of shopping,
you give into temptation. But once you are safely out of the environment and
reality kicks in ask yourself the following questions:

- Did you lower your standards because of a low price?

- Did you fall prey to shiny object syndrome?

- Did you purchase for the life you wish you had?

If you answer yes to any of these questions then promptly return the item.

You Were Settling

Sometimes you get frustrated when shopping because you can't find what
you really want or nothing works for you. This might happen after you've tried
on thirty pairs of jeans and you don't love any of them. You buy the pair that is
close enough just to get out of there.

Evaluate each purchase and honestly answer whether it meets your newly
raised standards. If not return it.

You Bought Wardrobe Orphans

When you love a piece and it fits perfectly but you never wear it you likely
have a wardrobe orphan. These are pieces that do not go with your other clothes,
shoes, and accessories.

Why might you buy such a piece? Perhaps you were thinking about your
fantasy life or you were trying out a new style. Sometimes, you don't realize right
away that you have a wardrobe orphan. You want to wear it but the opportunity

never arises. Or, you do go to wear it but you don't have the right shoes or undergarments.

Perhaps you are starting a new job and need some more business-like attire...

Maybe you want a fresh update...

Maybe you are overhauling or fine-tuning your wardrobe and realized you are missing some important pieces to make it work better for you...

What can you do?

Either return it or purchase the pieces needed to make it work.

When shopping, it's important to think about which existing clothes you have that will work well with any potential new purchase. In general, it's best to avoid buying pieces that are wardrobe orphans because there is a high risk that they will never get worn. But, there are always exceptions to any guidelines. There's a difference between buying wardrobe orphans for a fantasy life, and buying pieces to help to transition into a new career, retirement, a new hobby, or relocating to a new climate.

Seemed Good At First

Finally, there are the clothes, shoes, and accessories that you buy think-ing they are perfect. They are in your best shade, you want and need them, and you still love them during your post-purchase evaluation. However, when you try to wear them something is off.

Why?

Unfortunately, all the pre-planning and careful consideration in the world cannot identify all problems. Sometimes we don't realize there is an issue until we are wearing the piece for longer than five minutes. After a few hours, the issue becomes unbearable. All it takes is one or two things to turn something you thought would work for you into one that doesn't. Let's use handbags as an example.

There are so many decisions and considerations that go into buying a handbag. Issues most of us don't consider pre-purchase such as where it sits on body, if there enough compartments, and is it big enough?

For example, I ordered a bag online. I was in the market for a small cross body bag to wear while running errands. I've owned a few Coach bags so I know they are high quality. And, I figured I didn't have to worry about whether or not it would fit right. All these factors made me confident in my online purchase.

When the bag arrived it was gorgeous. I loved the vibrant red color. It sits nicely along my body and has an adjustable strap that I set to the perfect length. Plus, it is neither too bulky, nor too deep. However, I immediately took note that it was rather stiff. I figured, no big deal. It will soften as I use it.

But it hasn't.

I also realized rather quickly that it is actually just a tad too small because my sunglasses do not fit inside. My wallet takes up the entire interior compartment. Even after many uses, it is still rather stiff...

And the fact that it is just a tad too small is a constant annoyance...

I do use it every week for quick trips to the store but these issues haunt me every time I carry it.

Sometimes you can make it work

Yet another Coach handbag example. I received a beautiful blue tote bag as a gift. It was even reversible so one side was dark blue, the other light blue. But there were no interior compartments. None. Not even a small one for my keys or cell phone. I tried using it but was miserable. Everything ended up in a jumbled mess at the bottom of the bag. I didn't know what to do...

It was a gorgeous bag and I really wanted to carry it. In an effort to make it work I ordered a dark blue velvet purse interior compartment insert online. It was like magic! I suddenly loved the bag, and used it everyday for at least a year, if not longer.

Another gift was a beautiful pendant necklace which I had asked for. But the clasp was so tiny and delicate I could not for the life of me get it undone to put it on. Neither could anyone else. After finally getting it on with some help, trying to take it off was a nightmare. I thought I was going to have to break it or wear it forever!

The solution? I ordered magnetic necklace clasps online. They attach to the tiny clasp, so instead of fumbling with the tiny clasps I simply stick the magnets together. Attaching the magnetic claps to the necklace itself was a major struggle but I managed to get them on. Now I can easily put my necklace on and take it off with ease.

Sometimes you can't make it work.

We've all experienced the torture of those annoying fabric tags or labels. Some are like mini novels with several pages! They are long with sharp, scratchy corners. Shirt tags are something we often don't notice until we are out and about wearing the item and cannot change. You can try cutting the tag out but that can make the irritation even worse. Plus, you risk cutting the fabric. After many tag issues I now look for clothes that print the name into the fabric rather than attaching a paper novel inside.

Shoes are a category that if they pinch your feet because they are too tight, or you have blisters because they are too loose, you can't make it work. This can be a major problem since most stores will not accept returns once shoes have been worn. You can try wearing them around the house for several hours to ensure they fit properly. If they don't, you can return them.

Sometimes you use it but don't love it

Ok, I really do love Coach products! I got a beautiful blue pebbled leather Coach wallet that matched the reversible blue bag I just talked about. The problem? It had an all over zipper. I despise fussing with things and found it hard to unzip and rezip at the checkout. With that being said, I did use it for quite some time. When I was ready for a new wallet I made sure to get one with a snap open and close.

Post purchase satisfaction is the goal after every shopping trip. How do you set yourself up for post purchase satisfaction? You can use the knowledge and tools learned in this book to help you avoid post purchase dissonance and instead enjoy the delight of post purchase satisfaction. By doing your research before shopping and by being aware while shopping you increase your chances for a successful shopping trip.

We all make the occasional bad purchase, but that's no reason to berate ourselves. When you experience cognitive dissonance in the post purchase experience, examine why. Are you just panicking because you spent more than you planned? Or, should you return it because you secretly suspect you'll never wear it? Would an additional purchase make the item wearable? Why did you think you liked it at the store or online but now not so much?

If you do make a bad purchase, for whatever reason, it is imperative that you return the item as soon as possible. Returning items will help you get a wardrobe you love and that works for you. How? By reducing the number of unworn pieces in your closet, by eliminating guilt, and by freeing up funds for pieces you will love and that do work for you.

What's a surefire way to avoid post purchase dissatisfaction? A shopping slow down! Coming up next, we'll talk about the benefits of a shopping slow down and a purchasing pause.

Chapter 11

Shopping Slow Down

STOP STUFFING YOUR CLOSET

W e know we have way too many clothes, shoes, and accessories, yet we keep buying more. But why?

We are caught in a vicious cycle of dissatisfaction with our current wardrobe choices, shopping for something else, bringing it home, never wearing it, and wondering if we should have chosen something different. The dissatisfaction with our current wardrobe comes from both outside influences and our own internal pressure. As we learned throughout this book society, and particularly the fashion industry, wants us to buy, buy, and buy more. We feel pressured to always have the latest and the greatest, even if we don't want or need it. Designers and retailers lead us to believe we need a whole new wardrobe each season. But this endless pursuit of newer, better, and more is crazy, it's expensive, and excessive clothing purchases clog up your closet and contribute to wardrobe rage.

According to statistics, the average shopper visits a mall 2-3 times per month, stays for 80-135 minutes, and spends around $157. However, the longer you are at the mall, the more you tend to buy. Statistic also say that we only wear our garments on average 7 times and we wear 60% of our clothes for less than a year. Kind of crazy isn't it?

There will always be something else to buy. It's never-ending. And what are you buying? That shirt you must have is the same shirt hundreds and thousands of others have. Walk into any chain store and you will see the same pieces with a few exceptions based on climate and tone of the region. Whether you are in Pittsburgh or Panama City, you'll see the same pieces in the same stores. Why are we so compelled to buy these not-so-special pieces?

Did you really need that polyester blouse you got from the clearance rack at that discount store that you have never, ever worn, ever, ever, ever? Did you really need to buy that? Or did you just think you needed it or wanted it? Did you rationalize the purchase? Did you try to justify why you were willing to pay good money for it? Were you unable to resist the ridiculously low price? Were you shopping for retail therapy?

The majority of your wardrobe is not special. It is not unique. And it is not valuable. Sure, you might have a few designer handbags, some leather jackets, and some leather boots, but beyond that most of it is generic, run-of-the-mill, mass produced pieces. Because that's what most stores sell: generic, run-of-the-mill, mass produced pieces.

A continually rotating inventory is the business model for fast-fashion retailers like H&M, SHEIN and Boohoo. They get new pieces almost every day and expect consumers to discard their purchases after a short period of time. This is referred to as planned obsolescence. Fast fashion can also be called throwaway fashion. It's the practice of designing, manufacturing, and marketing items knowing they won't last long. The clothes are of poor quality and made from synthetic fabrics. They are trendy and quickly look dated. This creates a guarantee of recurring revenue because the customer has to keep buying more and more.

Excess shopping also leads to excess waste when we realize we are not wearing most of our wardrobe and we get rid of those items. Donation centers like Goodwill and The Salvation Army end up throwing out a large portion of their donations anyway because guess what? Those pieces you thought were so great but never wore, no one else wants them either. They end up as waste in landfills. This practice is turning the fashion industry into the second-largest polluter in the world.

Please don't let this discourage you from removing unworn items from your closet and donating them. The damage is already done. I'm sharing this so you think really hard before committing to upcoming purchases. If you don't buy it in the first place, you don't have to get rid of it. And if we, as a society, stop buying so much the fashion industry will stop producing so much. They don't want to deal with returns and unsold clothing either.

The bottom line is we really do shop too much and worry too much about clothes. Too much shopping inevitably leads to random purchases. Too many random purchases results in a stuffed closet full of mismatched items that don't work together. It's overwhelming. Just as the paradox of choice creates confusion when shopping, the same is true when trying to decide what to wear. There are just too many choices. In turn, this leads to wardrobe rage, analysis paralysis, depression, guilt, and too much wasted money. Yet, we keep adding more and more and more! How much is enough?

You willing pulled out your wallet and purchased every single thing. You put your new purchases into your already overflowing closet. But that isn't even the worst part. The bigger problem is most of them have stayed there since that day! What good is having five new shirts if you only wear one?

No one needs all these clothes. In fact, many people who could easily afford to change outfits several times each day without ever wearing anything twice make a conscious choice to rewear their clothes. Kate Middleton is a perfect example. She is often photographed wearing the same dress. And not just for daily wear. She repeats formal outfits too.

As we discussed in this book not all shopping is bad. It's important to stay current and to wear clothes without holes. But most of us only need a few new pieces each season to update worn-out pieces and to inject a little freshness.

There's a difference between focused shopping and random shopping.

Focused shopping is when you have a legitimate need, such as replacing pieces that are showing signs of wear. It can also be when you are on the hunt for something specific that you want, like a new handbag. There is absolutely nothing wrong with focused shopping.

Random shopping, on the other hand, can be a big problem. As we discussed in the *Misguided Motivation* chapter we often shop for reasons other than to buy clothes. We shop for entertainment, to curb boredom, to boost our mood, and to socialize. We want a new outfit to impress friends, co-workers, and even strangers. We hope our new clothes will help land us a mate, get us a new job or a promotion, or aid us in achieving a goal like losing weight.

Over-shopping constantly exposes you to the newest styles, to the on-trend colors, and to the so called must-haves. Looking at all the things for sale, the endless supply of clothes, shoes, and accessories available for purchase creates desire for these pieces. You discover things that you didn't know existed until you went shopping. Desire takes over your brain. The problems arise when there is no business aspect at all, just thoughtless buying. When it is all just search and conquer. Getting a haul. "Saving" money by buying clearance pieces.

What are some signs you shop too much?
- you have stacks of t-shirts, jeans, and sweaters that are constantly tumbling over

- you find it difficult to squeeze your arm between the rack of clothes

- you have lots of clothes you've never worn

- you have clothes with the tags still attached

- you aren't sure what all is in your closet

- you have trouble finding what you're looking for

- you are always up for a shopping trip

- you have retail websites bookmarked

- you have your credit card information stored on various online shopping sites

- you frequently regret your purchases

If any or all of these signs sounds familiar then I would like to introduce you to the concept of a shopping slow down. A shopping slowdown means:
- shopping less often

- shopping for shorter periods of time

- avoiding clothing and shoe stores for a few months

- buying fewer pieces per trip

- changing your mindset about shopping and your relationship with your clothes

- ensuring you like and wear your most recent purchases before buying more

- limiting online shopping by not visiting any clothing websites or clicking on ads

- ignoring coupons

- unsubscribing to clothing website emails

What are the benefits of a shopping slow down?

A shopping slow down benefits your wallet, your closet, and the planet. If that isn't enough motivation let me give you some more great reasons to shop less:

1. To spend less - the less you spend the more you save

2. To save money - instead of buying yet another pair of jeans how about saving that money, paying down debt, or putting it toward something special

3. To have less stuff - so you can stop fighting a losing battle with your closet

4. To have a functional closet - so you know what you have and can easily find it

5. To have clothes you like wearing - a closet full of clothes, shoes, and accessories that you really wear

6. To eliminate temptation - if you don't go shopping, you are not tempted

7. To stop chasing trends - fast fashion is typically poorly made and obsolete in a season or two

8. To create your own must-have list - you know what you like to wear so no need to follow someone else's dictates

9. To love your purchases - no more buying the wrong things

10. To not contribute to harming the environment - fewer purchases means fewer pieces in landfills

A shopping slowdown allows you to become more aware of what you are wearing and what you already have. A shopping slow down can also mean taking the time to be sure it works. Don't keep buying more clothes until you've worn your most recent purchases. Remember: if you don't keep adding the wrong pieces to your wardrobe, you won't have to keep purging so much. It also makes getting dressed easier, faster, and less stressful.

A shopping slowdown, combined with focused shopping when you do shop, will result in a well curated wardrobe that you love to wear. When you shift from random over-shopping, to shopping less often with purpose and intention, it's actually more fun, more productive and more satisfying. These are all reasons why I would like you to consider a shopping slow down.

There are many courses and challenges out there that encourage you to take a year off from clothes shopping or to avoid the mall for a month. While these can be beneficial in the short term, I encourage you to look at this as a lifestyle change rather than a temporary hiatus. Why? Because we all need to shop for clothes occasionally. That's why you need to train yourself to shop with restraint. A shopping slow down does you no good if you revert back to your old ways.

How can you initiate a shopping slow down?

It won't work if you simply say, "I'm going to slow down my shopping." Why not?

Because it's just a general statement. There are no parameters or guidelines. If you shop online every day a slow down could mean shopping every other day. That is still too much. You need to define what a slow down looks like for you. If you go to the mall at least once a month try cutting back to just once or twice a season. Use this as your benchmark. If you look online every day or several times per week, cut back. Look once per week or once per month.

To cut back on your shopping learn to identify your shopping triggers. When you get the urge to go shopping question why. Do you truly need something or are you bored, upset, or trying to fill a void? Just because you get the urge to shop that does not mean you must give in. Any time you feel the urge to shop take a look at your closet. Do you really want to put more clothes, shoes, and accessories in there?

Ask yourself, how much is enough?

How many more clothes does one person need?

Think about the real cost of your clothes both in terms of money spent and time wasted. Money wasted on clothes your don't love, don't need, and don't wear. Time wasted shopping for those clothes. Time wasted digging through your packed closet looking for something that fits, that is appropriate for your day, and that you like.

Practice the Purchasing Pause

When you do shop and are on the verge of buying another shirt, pair of shoes, or a dress stop and take a purchasing pause. Think long and hard about whether you really need to add another piece of clothing to your wardrobe. Use the information you've learned throughout this book to make better choices or to not buy anything at all. Question whether you are caving to one or more of your personal purchasing triggers.

Think about the big picture.

Remember the real cost of your clothes.

Pay attention to how much you are *spending* rather than focusing on how much you are *saving* with a coupon or by purchasing a markdown.

Think about how much you will *save* if you didn't purchase the item at all.

And consider how much extra you will actually be spending if you charge pieces and don't pay the bill immediately thus accruing interest.

What could you do with the money you are about to spend on clothes? Put it in savings? Use it for something you really want and will really love?

I've saved the topic of a shopping slowdown for the end of this book because you are now better informed and in a different mindset about your wardrobe. The thing is there will always be something you will want. Long after you've forgotten about one thing, another will take it's place.

You need clothes...

And it's nice to wear new things...

But there are other things to do with your money. There is more to life than clothes.

After reading this book you *WILL SHOP SMARTER*. When you do *DECIDE* to go shopping because you have a legitimate *NEED* you will be *FOCUSED*. You can *AVOID* everything you *DO NOT NEED*.

No more, I came for shoes but let me just check out the jackets.

Or, I can't find what I *need* so let me find something I *want*.

Shop less often.

Practice a purchasing pause before pulling out that pocketbook. Think through each and every purchase.

Keep your receipts and the tags on until you actually wear it.

If you decide you should have left it at the store, take it back!

Chapter 12

A New Approach

FINAL TIPS TO ENSURE SUCCESS

C ongratulations! After reading this book you now have the knowledge you need to enjoy shopping by making it more successful. From now on you will start treating your wardrobe and yourself with respect and importance.

You learned how to shop with purpose, how to spend wisely, and how to ensure successful shopping trips.

You know how to identify your shopping triggers and habits making you well equipped to combat them.

You realize the benefits of raising your standards and being clear about what you are really shopping for.

You've learned methods to help you rethink how you shop for clothes.

Before you step foot in a mall or start shopping online determine why you are shopping. Remember the chapter *Misguided Motivation?* What problem are you trying to solve with the purchase of new clothes, shoes, or accessories. Is it an identified need because something is missing from your current wardrobe? Or, are you just shopping for something to do? Again, there is nothing wrong with the occasional trip to check out the new arrivals or for entertainment. As long as you are aware and prepared to keep a tight reign on your wallet.

With so many options it's beneficial to create a shopping strategy or a game plan. While you will still be faced with many obstacles, distractions, buying triggers, and emotions while shopping, detailed planning will help immensely. Having a list of specific items to look for, as well as a predetermined budget, will help you avoid falling victim to shiny object syndrome and the lure of a low price. It will help reduce the decision fatigue, analysis paralysis, confusion, overwhelm, and shopping rage we talked about earlier. Making decisions in advance about what you will focus on on and where you will go reduces decision fatigue and overwhelm.

Look at the mall website directory beforehand to get a feel for the layout and the locations of specific stores. Take note of the entrances, the restrooms, and the food court. Plan where to park, which door to enter, and which route to take once inside. Pre-shop the websites of the stores you are unfamiliar with but that you think might work for you. You'll get an overview of the types of clothes they offer, as well as their pricing.

Before committing to any purchase take a pause. Really think about whether you need and want any potential purchase. Going forward, you will think about how much you are spending versus how much you could save *without* buying something. Picture the large number of clothes you already have and whether you want to add to it with this choice. Does it meet all of your criteria? Do you love it?

Shift the focus from spending to save, to saving by not spending. Every time you see the word *save* associate it with the *action of spending*. Unless the word *save* is being used to talk about putting money in a savings account, *associate it with spending.*

Do you really need another pair of sneakers?

Do you really need another t-shirt?

And do you really need another pair of jeans?

In most cases, the answer is a hard no.

When you do buy clothes, shoes, and accessories it is vital to reevaluate your purchases when you return home. Once the shopping high is gone see if you still like everything. Make sure each piece meets your high standards, as well as works with the rest of your wardrobe.

No one knows how much or how little you paid for something unless you tell them. You may think you are smart getting a steal. But the joke is on you if it is not flattering or it just sits in your closet. Being smug about "getting a steal" is the wrong way to go.

How about being smug about your great purchase that you love, that fits you perfectly, that you want and need, and that works with the rest of your wardrobe and for your lifestyle? People don't look at you and wonder how much you paid for what you are wearing. They just notice whether or not you look good and whether or not your clothes fit.

Below are some final thoughts to keep in mind when it comes to shopping for clothes.

Shopping is hard work

It takes patience, perseverance and planning.

Raise your standards

Be ruthless in your pursuit of what you want, need, and like. Do not lower your standards for a low price! You shouldn't have to talk yourself into a purchase. Instead of looking for bargains, start looking for quality.

Don't rush it

Realize it takes time to build your wardrobe. It takes time to get it even close to how you want it. Even those with unlimited funds or a generous wardrobe budget should take it slow and easy.

Stick to your style

This helps you to avoid the pressure of buying fleeting trends. Don't fall prey to fashion magazine's must have lists and latest styles.

Have a shopping strategy

Shop strategically with purpose and a plan. Make a list of what you need and want, create a budget, and stick to it.

Keep your goals in mind

Remember to ask yourself: do I want to save money, or do I want to look the best I can and feel as confident as possible? Invest in yourself. You are totally worth it!

Don't trust salespeople

Their title says it all, "sales" Their job is to sell, especially those who work on commission. Stores stay in business because we consume so much. They want us to believe we need more, more, more...

A bargain is no bargain if you never wear it or use it

Instead, it is the complete opposite: a waste of money.

Quality is key

Still strive for well-made, high quality pieces regardless of the price point. There are inexpensive well-made pieces. And there are expensive poorly made pieces. Pay attention to the fabric and construction.

Track your purchases

Keep track of what you buy, where you buy it, and how much you spend. This alone can cause you to pause before a purchase. It can also be a real eye-opener.

Don't blow your budget

Don't waste your money on impulse purchases and a bunch of trendy items. Spread your budget out over the entire year by breaking it down by the four seasons, by warm weather and cold weather, or by lifestyle category.

Don't spend to save

Don't think about it as not getting that new sweater. Think about how much money you'll retain by admiring the sweater but leaving it at the store because you already have ten sweaters that you rarely even wear.

Save by not buying

Learn to walk away. It's tough but you must do it. Even if it is just leaving the store for a half hour. Once you get away from the situation you often rethink the purchases. Maybe you will go back and just buy one of the pieces instead of four. Or maybe you don't go back at all.

Resist temptation

You may love the look or the idea of slinky dresses or power suits but the reality is you have no occasion to wear them. Stick to pieces that you need for you current lifestyle.

Know your weaknesses

Be aware of styles you find hard to resist and enjoy buying the most. Steer clear of them when shopping for other items that you need and do not already have in abundance.

Know what you don't like

Trying to force yourself to wear anything is a surefire way to ensure you never wear it. If you love t-shirts and jeans, and don't need to dress up for work, don't buy business style clothes. You do not have to wear dresses, skirts, and heels if you don't want to. If you hate button up blouses, don't buy any. Instead, look for camisoles or silk t-shirts if you need something a step up from a cotton t-shirt.

Slow down

Shop less. Spend more time thinking about each purchase. Stop adding more to your already full closet.

Success is not measured by the extent of your wardrobe.

Besides, you prefer to be smart with your money. You have other things to buy besides more clothes. You have other priorities like saving money, buying a house, or taking a trip.

More is not better, it is just more

The more you own the less you appreciate it.

The less you own the more you appreciate it.

Shop Smarter. Look Better. Love Your Wardrobe.

Chapter 13

Stages of Shopping

FROM START TO FINISH

The consumer shopping process begins before you leave the house. It is the series of stages we experience before we shop, while shopping online or in person, and after we return home. Below are the shopping stages you go through and the questions you should be asking to ensure you curate a wardrobe that works for you!

Stage #1: Problem recognition - you are starting to see the symptoms of a problem brewing such as:

- you don't have the right shoes to wear with skirts or trousers

- you notice your work clothes are looking dreary and worn

- you realized your winter jacket is not warm enough after freezing the last few times you wore it

- you don't have any casual sandals to wear to the beach or pool

- your favorite sweater has a few holes

- you struggle to get dressed for work, to work out, or to run to the store

- you struggle to find clothes to wear around the house that don't make you feel like a slob

Stage #2: Information gathering - you start to think about how you can solve your wardrobe problems by:

- identifying the pieces that are missing from your wardrobe

- researching current styles for the activities for which you need clothes

- researching looks you like and evaluating the elements of those looks

- thinking about which retailers and brands are likely to have what you're looking for

Stage #3: Evaluating solutions - getting more specific, narrowing down options and choices, ruling some options out

- cost - establishing a budget based on how much can you afford to spend and how much are you prepared to spend

- preparation – making a detailed wants and needs list

- most urgent – which pieces are priorities and which can wait

- brand - which brands have worked well for you in the past, which brands do you want to check out

- where to shop - which stores, malls, and websites might have what you need

Stage #4: Purchase phase - shopping for and committing to a decision

- will these new purchases make your wardrobe more functional and better

- is the shade flattering

- does it fit properly

- does this work for your lifestyle

- does this fit your personal style

- is it well-made and of high quality

- what is the estimated cost-per-wear

- does it meet you high standards

- does this solve your wardrobe dilemma

Stage #5: Post-purchase phase - reevaluating your purchases once you get home

- do you still like it as much as you thought you did at the store

- does it look like it goes with your other clothes

- does the color work with your existing wardrobe

- are you comfortable with how much you spent

- are you excited to wear it

- did you make a mistake and should you return it

Thank You For Reading

I hope this book helps you to shop smarter and love your clothes.

If you didn't already, be sure to download your FREE An Imperfect Purchase Workbook.

You can also get the FREE Workbook at https://closetcures.com/workbook-an-imperfect-purchase/

I really appreciate your feedback, and I love hearing how An Imperfect Purchase has helped you make clothing choices that work for you and your lifestyle.

Could you leave me a review on Amazon letting me know what you thought of the book?

Thank you so much! You can find even more information about shopping smarter on my website: https://closetcures.com/

Be sure to email me with any questions or comments at lindawolfe@closetcures.com

About the Author

Linda is a wardrobe strategist and the creator of https://closetcures.com/ where she helps women and men curate a wardrobe that works for them. She has a bachelor's degree in Fashion Merchandising, a master's degree in Asset and Property Management with a concentration on retail stores and shopping centers, and a certificate from *The Image Maker, Inc* program for image consultants. Linda reads every style and image book she can find. Through her many years of education, research, career experience, and personal experience, Linda has come to understand why we have so many clothes we never wear and what we can do about it.

Also By Linda Wolfe

AN IMPERFECT WARDROBE

An Imperfect Wardrobe by Linda Wolfe

Are you on a never-ending quest to get the perfect wardrobe?

Have you done what you were "supposed to do" and bought the pieces you were "supposed to buy" only to find yourself more confused and overwhelmed than before...

And instead of getting a perfect wardrobe you have a closet crammed full of clothes, shoes, and accessories that you never wear and don't really even like...

If you're tired of wasting your precious time and hard-earned money on your wardrobe **then this is the book for you!**

In *An Imperfect Wardrobe* you'll learn how to focus on slowly curating a closet filled with clothes, shoes, and accessories that work for **your lifestyle, your budget, and your personal preferences.** This is the ultimate practical guide packed with tactics to help you stop the struggle, streamline your wardrobe, and take back control of your closet.

In this book we'll tackle questions like:

- How your mindset impacts the state of your wardrobe, for better and for worse

- Why parting with unworn clothes is so hard, and how to do it anyway

- How many clothes do you really need, and does it even matter

- Why you just had to have it, but never wear it

- How to shop smarter, so you buy clothes you'll actually enjoy wearing

After reading *An Imperfect Wardrobe* you will finally understand why you have been at war with your wardrobe and what you can do about it.

Including the **free downloadable bonus *An Imperfect Wardrobe Workbook*** filled with printable worksheets, checklists, and guides to keep you on track, eliminate buying mistakes, and help you realize your unique wardrobe goals.

Remember: your wardrobe doesn't have to be perfect. It just has to work for you! Because you have better things to do than stress about your clothes.

Are you ready to:

- uncover the roadblocks that stop you from getting rid of clothes you don't wear

- figure out why you're buying the wrong clothes in the first place

- and curate a purchasing plan for future shopping trips?

Then let's get started...

Printed in Great Britain
by Amazon